About this book

This book contains ecological field studies techniques, that can be conducted in wild nature by non-professional researchers - school and university students together with their teachers, single beginning investigators, families, amateurs of all ages.

The whole book "Investigating Nature Together" includes 4 parts/series corresponding to a specific season (Autumn-Winter-Spring-Summer) with totally 40 environmental study lessons covered a wide variety of activities in nature which focus on aquatic ecology, botany, forest ecology, soil studies, landscape analysis, ornithology, anthropogenic effects on nature, etc.

Each series contains lessons focusing on practical skills which will be applied in further field studies. The lessons focus on five main themes; landscape, botany, zoology, water ecology and environmental monitoring. Some lessons are closely associated with the seasons and others are more universal.

This book promotes a wide variety of outcomes which correspond to established educational standards in many countries. The ecological field study activities address content standards in the areas of earth science, life science, biology, ecology and the nature of science. Intellectual skill development includes questioning, data collection, analysis and drawing conclusions. Affective outcomes include an appreciation for the processes of science, the use of technology in basic scientific endeavors and a greater value of natural, scientific and cultural systems.

This book promotes understanding of ecosystems and the protection of the environment through the training of teachers in specific field study techniques, the education of young people in ecology concepts and issues and the sharing of ecological study results between colleagues. The primary goal of this work is connecting students and teachers, addressing important environmental issues and promoting environmental interest, knowledge and values.

This book is addressed to the middle and secondary level science teachers and students, and for all those who would like to investigate local wild nature, to share ecological and cultural information and work together to help create a better environment.

This specific book **"Investigating Nature Together. Part 2: Winter"** is the second in the series. It includes several typical winter investigations which take advantage of seasonal characteristics including low temperatures and snow. These include: mammal behavior based on snow tracks, snow strata study and chickadee territoriality. However, we have included some lessons which are more universal and lab oriented taking into consideration that outside studies can be more difficult in winter conditions. Lessons continue to develop and extend previous skills related to mapping.

The techniques described in this book, were written by Alexander Bogolyubov (1996-2002), translated into English by Tatiana Tatarinova (2002) and edited by Michael Brody (2003). They have been translated in English and edited for the distance Ecological Field Techniques Course, offered through Montana State University in 2003-2007.

The list of all 40 field study lessons:

I. Autumn season:

1.   Orientation to Local Habitat and Study Site
2.   Description of Geological Exposure
3.   Profile of River Valley Slope
4.   Soil Profile Pit
5.   Forest Health Based on Observations of Coniferous Trees
6.   Species Composition and Abundance of Fungi
7.   Census of Birds Using Line Transect Counting Method
8.   Integrated Study of Landscape Profile
9.   Environmental Assessment of Human Impact
10. Assessment of Air Pollution Using Lichen Bioindication

II. Winter season (this book):

1.   Making a Fire for Winter Survival
2.   Simple Survey of Field Study Site
3.   Growth Dynamics of Trees
4.   Forest Mapping
5.   Green Plants under Snow Cover
6.   Territorial Behavior of Titmouse Flocks
7.   Winter Route Census of Mammals
8.   Mammal Ecology According to Winter Tracking
9.   Physical and Chemical Properties of Natural Waters
10. Snow Cover Profile

III. Spring season:

1.   Helping Native Birds
2.   Early Flowering Plants

3. Spring Flowers

4. Vital State of Coniferous Underbrush

5. Forest Invertebrates (Part 1)

6. Amphibians

7. Rocks and Minerals

8. Daily Bird Song Activity

9. Bird Census Methods

10. Fauna of Vernal Pools

IV. Summer season:

1. School Herbarium

2. Flora Inventory

3. Vertical Structure of a Forest

4. Forest Invertebrates (Part 2)

5. Birds Nesting Behavior

6. Comparative Description of Small Rivers and Streams

7. Aquatic Invertebrates and Environmental Status

8. Plankton in the Littoral Zone of a Water-body

9. Environmental Status of Meadows

10. Status of Forests Based on Asymmetry of Tree Leaves

If you have any questions or need an advice on the lessons below, write to ecosystema1994@yandex.ru.

Making a Campfire

This manual describes the rules of choosing a campfire site, the technique for starting the bonfire and preparation of fuel in field conditions. The manual describes different types of bonfires used for different purposes. The activity is arranged in a form of a game with elements of competition .

Introduction

This activity begins a series of studies devoted to the organization of students' research in winter. However, as with lessons from other seasons, the series begins not with research itself, but with **practical activities***. In this case the activities are aimed at fire- making skills and camp construction in field conditions. It is possible that the skills students acquire in the course of the given lesson will prove useful in following activities, i.e. when organizing ecological field studies in the course of a camping trip and expedition that lasts several days.

---

* **Bold** = important text phrases, ***Bold/Italic*** = key vocabulary, *Italic* = examples and specific illustrations.

The general plan of the activity

Because the lesson is not specifically oriented to scientific research, we recommend it as a single day activity in the form of a game with elements of competition.

During the **first stage** of the activity, the teacher explains and demonstrates the guidelines for choosing a temporary site for a fire, the technique of setting the fire, methods of preparing fuel and various types of fires.

The second stage of the activity is the competition to start the fire. For this purpose, it is best to take students to the forest where there is fuel and it is possible to make a camp fire at the end of the day and to seat together after the competition.

At the field site we recommend that the group be divided into pairs. Each pair is given five matches and the task to start the fire as quickly as possible. Each group must choose a site for their fire, collect fuel and start the fire so that it will not die out. It must be done quickly and with use of the least number of matches. If a group uses all their matches the teacher may gives them another five, and so on until the fire starts.

After the competition all fires must be safely extinguished.

In this field activity a **class report** is appropriate. The report may include the results of the competition (amount of time and number of matches for each group of students), 2-3 pictures of students during the most important or funny episodes of the day and pictures of different types of fires made by students.

What is a bonfire?

Hence, the present manual is not a manual according to its purpose, but it relates some rules of organization for camping and expedition life. Unlike all the other manuals for the educational activities of the given series it has been completely adopted from master campers and enthusiastic hikers (G.Ya. Ryzhavsky, 1995). The author is an experienced traveler, a master of sports in this field and a man of humor. We consider this text, which he has written about fires, to almost completely satisfy our ideas of the fire building aspects of hiking trips or field research, so we inserted it into the given manual almost without changes.

If you announced a contest of the best camping emblem, undoubtedly, a fire would be that emblem. In one recording, where "all campers' wisdom" is collected, it is explained that " . . . a bonfire is a contrivance designed for campers' warming, cooking and drying of wet clothes." Even a staunch pragmatist would not feel any interest in hiking after having read such a definition. It is possible to cook, get warm and dry wet clothes at home! Therefore, a bonfire is more than just a flame. It is the center of a camp (bivouac). The bonfire is kitchen, dining room and sitting room. It means dry clothes and hot water, protection from horseflies and other bloodsuckers; it is a place of communication, and it is heat and comfort.

Moreover, the bonfire is an accumulator of cheerfulness, energy and activities. No trips or hiking tours in forested areas are without a fire. The bonfire is a reliable friend of the camper. One is to treat it skillfully and with respect. If it is treated carelessly, it can become a cruel thief. Fires can be dangerous! So, a **fire is an emblem and a symbol**. And a symbol should be held in high respect!

Site for the bonfire

What does any **bonfire begin** with? It begins with a site. If the camping site is narrow and uncomfortable then the bonfire site is given the best place in the camp as the beloved but fretful child.

The **bonfire should be placed** not high and not low, not far away and not close. It should light up all the tents if possible and its smoke should disperse mosquitoes throughout the whole camping site, and the fire itself should produce enough heat for all the members of the group plus three cauldrons or buckets. However, it can be dangerous if sparks from the fire do not have enough time to "die out in the air" and reach a tent. It is not good if the smoke chokes not only mosquitoes but humans as well.

The code of rules on how to choose a **proper site** for the bonfire is serious science, but it is an art to put them into practice! It is advisable to select a site for the bonfire at an open place that is protected from the wind and is close to water. Wind can set fire to grass, brushwood and dry leaves while it fans the flame. Fire can spread along dry grass very fast. In such cases it is recommended not to place many logs into the campfire and to limit the size of the flame. It is better to make a bonfire at an old fireplace or on a trampled sand-site, where grass and fertile topsoil will not be burned down. It is advised to take turf away at the place of the campfire, so that it can be put back later. Dry leaves, grasses, branches and needles, which can easily catch fire, should be raked away from the fire site.

Do not make a bonfire under trees, especially dried out ones. Fire can destroy the roots of the tree and burn its lower dry branches. It is dangerous to build a fire in young coniferous forest areas or at sites with the presence of dry rush, reed, moss or dry grass, because the fire spreads along them very fast. Campfires at lumber clearings are also dangerous as ignition of dried out remains of felling operations can cause forest fires. It is also prohibited to make bonfires on peat bogs, as even an extinguished and put out fire can smolder imperceptibly for a long time within the lower turf layer and cause a big fire in several days. At the worst, a bonfire can be built on a "pillow" made of earth and sand, which has been scattered on the peat bog.

The site for the bonfire in winter is selected so that warm air currents do not reach snow-covered branches. Otherwise, when the bonfire flares up, it and people standing around it will be poured with a rain called "kukhta", caused by melting snow on tree branches.

If there is deep snow it is necessary to make a flooring of live logs for the bonfire. The duckrun should then be placed on two transverse pieces of deadwood. If the snow cover is not deep, it is possible to clear a fire site of snow down to the ground.

Upon leaving the campsite, do not be lazy. Douse the fire with water even if there are no smoldering embers or coals. This rule should always be observed. The main reason for most great forest fires is still badly extinguished bonfires.

Setting on fire

Everybody knows that it is preferable to light a bonfire with the help of

only one match. It is also known that a squanderer who wastes two matches does not deserve to be called "a camper." It would be interesting to know when the legend about masters who always set fire with the help of only one match first appeared! As in all legends, it is also very inspiring. So I will not dissuade you from good intentions to make a fire with the help of one match when it rains. Quite the contrary, I have to encourage you: "Dare to dream!"

Meanwhile, there are several methods that can sharply reduce the number of matches required for fire making. Inexperienced campers would hasten to say: "petrol or gasoline!" OK, next time, try it and take a bottle with kerosene with you. Two hours into the trip, there won't be a single object left that doesn't smell of kerosene. All foodstuffs will absorb the smell of fuel. Even canned meat that's just been opened will smell like a gas station. There is also a wonderful method using dry alcohol. Unfortunately this material is very hygroscopic, meaning it absorbs moisture and turns into mush. That is why there are no methods better than the old barbarian one: to increase combustion rate with the help of paper or a candle-end.

I can give you one more piece of advice. It *is* possible to kindle wet firewood, but first, it is quite difficult, and second, dry firewood will still be required for further fire making. That is why we recommend that all of you to hide some dry tree branches inside the tent before going to bed. They can be wrapped in cellophane.

Now let's talk about matches. Matches for fire making should certainly be dry. They can be kept dry even in wet clothes or camping gear if they are glued up or wrapped into polyethylene film. Boxes of matches can be taken in unsealed paper bags during simple and winter hiking trips. It is possible to try to dry out damp matches. If they get wet but do not become limp, they can be dried out in the sunlight or even in one's hair under a hat. Matches should be kept in waterproof packing in the course of water-related trips. Each hiker should have an emergency stock, for example, a hermetically sealed box of matches (in a weather-proof-jacket or in a special bag), as the hiker as well as his or her things can fall into water. Matches for everyday use can be kept unsealed. However, each professional hiker always keeps the matches dry.

It is very difficult to start a fire if there are no of matches, even if a person masters all the wisdom of life in the Stone Age. It is possible to strike a fire with the help of flint, fire-steel and by rubbing. It is very difficult to make a fire by rubbing, but it is possible when necessary. In order to do that, one must make a bow out of a birch or filbert branch one meter long and 2-3 cm thick and a piece of a string used as a bow-string. A drill is made out of a pine stick 25-30 cm long, which is as thick as a pencil. The stick should be pointed at one end. A prop (fire base) can be made of a dry log of hard-grained trees (birch, oak, etc.), which should be debarked and a hole of 1-1.5 cm deep cut out with the help of a knife. The drill is wrapped round once with a bowstring, and it is placed with its sharp end into the hole, where tinder (dry string, tow and wadding) is put around it. The drill is pressed with a left hand through lining (made of tree bark, fabric, mittens and so on), and then the bow is moved back and forth transversely to the drill. As soon as the tinder starts smoldering it should be fanned and put into prepared kindling (cotton wool, piece of rotten wood, etc.).

On a sunny day, fire can be obtained with the help of a burning-glass, which focuses solar rays upon cotton wool, a piece of paper, etc. The lenses of cameras, glasses or binoculars can be used instead of a burning glass.

It is best to make the bonfire according to the following procedure: First, it is necessary to set fire to kindling (any ignitable material such as birch bark from fallen or dead trees, paper, thin dry wood chips, thin dry twigs, or a candle). The kindling should be set on the fire from the bottom, or it will burn out completely. The kindling will pass the fire to dry twigs, chips and splinters, which have to be piled in the form of a hut. It should then be covered with thicker twigs, and then you can put thicker branches. At last you can put the thickest branches and firewood. There should be gaps left among twigs, chips and firewood in order to allow air to come in to the fire. If you pack firewood very closely into a weak bonfire, the fire can die out. At the beginning it is necessary to make sure that all firewood is dry, otherwise it will not burn: as there won't be enough heat for the drying and kindling of old logs. In the beginning, do not put thick logs into the bonfire, because they may not have enough time to catch fire (there is not enough heat), whereas thinner branches will be burned down. Increase the thickness of logs gradually and you will get the desired fire.

Kindling can be placed directly on the dry ground in summer; in winter it should be placed on a flooring of logs stowed closely together, and it is better to use damp logs. Do not start to make fire until you stock enough firewood to begin with, otherwise, the bonfire will die out and you will have to start from the beginning again. Once coals are formed in the bonfire, it will not die out easily. By adding the firewood gradually, you can maintain a desired intensity of fire.

It is much more difficult to make a **bonfire in the rain**. It is necessary to get well prepared, as a carelessly made fire will easily die out. It is recommended to have an artificial piece of kindling (pieces of candles, pellets of dry alcohol) in order to start the bonfire in rain. It is possible to plane some chips for kindling with the help of a knife, as even dry coniferous needles have some wet surfaces in the rain. Chips and cuttings will easily catch fire from the kindling. Thicker branches should be split, as they are quite dry inside. It is suggested to stretch an awning above the bonfire or you can just protect it with the polyethylene or place it under the canopy of an awning.

Some campers who get wet in the rain put up their tents in a hurry, hide inside and do not want to get out again, preferring not to cook, and spend their entire time inside tents. Do not be deterred; make the bonfire in the rain! It will elevate the team's mood, provide an opportunity to cook food, dry up supplies and clothes, and warm team members so all get a good rest.

Fuel for the bonfire

Use dry brushwood and dry tree branches for the bonfires, and deadwood in winter.

Large bonfires are harmful and unnecessary. They require a lot of firewood, it is impossible to cook on them, and it is difficult to dry clothes with them. Moreover, the bonfire "up to heaven" is dangerous. Dry trees standing at any distance can catch fire with the help of wind; firebrands can fly out and set fire to grass and brushwood far from the bonfire. Such bonfire can easily get out of hand.

When in the vicinity of human settlements or populated areas only the fuels that cannot be used by the local people, i.e. small brushwood, dry crooked trees, felling debris and old stumps, should be used to make a bonfire. Firewood can be purchased from a forester or campers can take primus (kerosene) stoves or gas stoves with them. However, there is always enough brushwood and deadwood in the taiga that is far from human settlements.

It is well known that damp wood and spunk burn with much smoke, whereas small brushwood burns down quite fast. Large intense bonfire can be made mainly of pine, spruce and cedar deadwood.

In forest poor areas, a bonfire will require an economical spending of firewood and sensitivity towards vegetation. Fireplaces for bonfires in the steppe are made of turf, whereas in mountains they are made of stones. The fire will produce more heat if the distance between the sidewalls of the fireplace is wider from the windward side than from the leeward side. Dry bushes, grass, pressed dung and rush can serve as fuel.

If the bonfire needs to burn all the night long in order to warm sleeping campers, then it is necessary to distribute duties, otherwise sleeping people will be threatened with sparks and coals which can fall on them and their sleeping bags. The fire should be watched constantly even if it burns down.

High trees should not be cut down if it is not necessary: It is laborious and dangerous work. Thick logs for the bonfire are required only in winter. Fallen trees are usually very damp in winter, as fallen trunks are covered with snow, whereas in autumn they become wet in the rain. They are usually not lighted by the sun or blown around by the wind.

A tree should be felled to the side of its natural leaning, but you should check whether it would hang on another tree while falling. **Do not** try to **fell** the tree **against** its obvious **incline**. It is difficult and dangerous. First, make a notch of one third or one fourth of the trunk diameter into the side where the tree will fall.

Then notch the tree from the opposite side, higher than the first notch. Notches made with the help of an axe should be deep enough. It is easier to fell trees by making saw cuts with the help of a two-handled or even a single-handled saw. The gash of one half of the trunk diameter should be made on the side to where the tree will fall. Then chip above the gash and take the wedge out with the help of an axe or a saw. The second gash should be made on the opposite side, which will be approximately 5 cm higher than the first one. Before that you should make sure that you can freely move aside when the tree falls. When the second gash meets the first one, it is necessary to push the tree with a pole and to let it fall.

When the tree starts falling, you should be very careful: it can rebound back, especially if you fell it with the help of an axe. The tree bends when falling down and breaks off a chip, which can spring and throw the trunk back to the side where the tree-cutters stand. So when the second gash starts split on its own, all people who are not engaged in felling should move away to a distance longer than the tree height. In winter, tree-cutters should take off their skis and tread out a path in the snow for possible escape if the tree starts falling on them.

Put your tree or limb on a log or a beam when you chop firewood. Do not chop it on the ground or on stones. It is not recommended to use a foot to hold the tree that you are chopping, as the foot is too close to the place where the axe lands. It is better to saw thick logs. If you hold the log with your foot, then you should not put it directly in front of you, but to one side. The notch should be made on the opposite side of the log from where you stand.

Types of bonfires

Sometimes bonfires are classified into "smoke" fires (for signaling, deterrence of mosquitoes, horse-flies and midges), "heat" fires (designed for cooking, drying clothes and warming people, especially if they sleep near the bonfire) and "flaming" fires (to light up the camp and to be used for cooking). There are also some main types of bonfires according to their structure; however, each of the bonfire types according to any classification is rarely strictly applied.

The "Hut" or "Cone" (number 1 on the picture). Logs are placed or put at an angle to the center. Sometimes they partly lean against each other. The fire will be concentrated and hot in the upper part of the bonfire. This bonfire is useful for lighting of the camping site and for cooking with a small number of pots. Brushwood, fallen branches and other thin logs can be used for this type.

The bonfire will produce high fire, but it is characterized with a narrow heating zone, it produces little smoke and it requires constant addition of fuel.

The "Well" is a heating bonfire (2). Two logs are placed on the coals parallel to each other at a certain distance; two other logs should be laid down across them and so on. There is good air access within the bonfire; logs usually burn evenly along the full length. They burn down slowly and produce much coal, giving high temperature. This bonfire is useful for cooking, and warming up, and drying clothes.

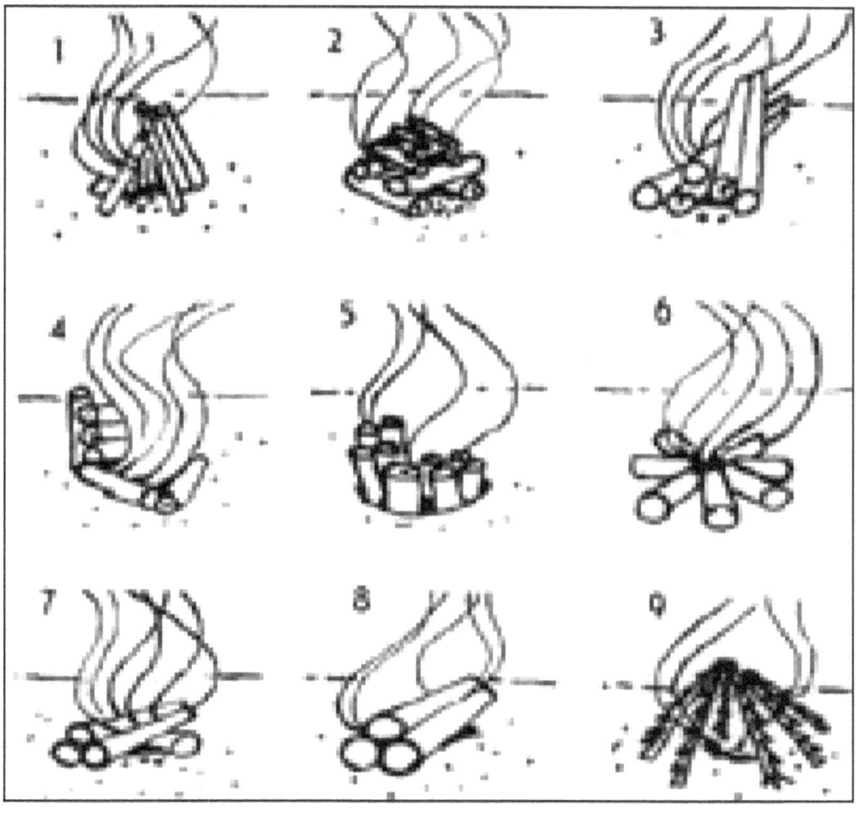

The "Star" (6). Logs (5-6 pieces) are placed on coals from several sides along radiuses out from the center. It burns mainly in the center. Logs should be moved as they burn down.

So-called **"Taiga"** (3) bonfires have several varieties. For instance, a row of long logs (2 or 3) is placed on the same row lengthwise or at a certain angle. The fire burns above coals and at places, where rows cross. Three logs can be put closely or almost next to each other. The bonfire will burn along the full length, especially at places where logs adjoin. There is one more type of bonfire: thick logs are placed among coals. Other logs are placed on them with one end, and a pile of coals is found under them.

The extended front of the fire on such a bonfire allows for cooking food for a large team, as well as drying clothes and spending nights without a tent near the bonfire. This is a long-term bonfire; it does not require frequent addition of firewood.

"Nod'ya" (8). Logs of the same length and thickness are prepared for this bonfire. It is recommended to use pine, spruce or cedar logs. Two logs are placed close to each other on the ground. Kindling or coals from the other bonfire is placed in the gap between logs, then a third log is placed on top. Kindling can be put between two logs which lay one on top of the other, so you have to trim the lower log and hammer four stakes-supports in the corners in order to hold the upper log. Nod'ya flames gradually and burns with a steady hot flame for several hours. It is possible to regulate the bonfire by parting and pushing together the logs, or in the case of a log lying on top of another, by moving aside the third log that is an air regulator.

The following types of bonfires are also recommended: "**Fireplace**" (4), "**Polynesian**" (5), and "**Gun**" (7). If there is little firewood, than it is possible to build "fireplace" of stones or damped logs: food can be quickly cooked on it.

The aforementioned types of bonfires are just basic constructions; they are rarely applied just as they are. At the beginning the bonfire can have a shape of a "**Hut**" (9) or a well, then logs are placed in different combinations. "The hut", "the well" and the "taiga" bonfires can be used in order to set a fire; small chips and twigs can be put this way.

Each camper finds his or her own favorite type of bonfire and procedure of fire making as they gain experience. The general principle of fire setting and its maintenance consists in the regulation of the quantity and quality of fuel and size of gaps between logs and firewood. Larger or smaller fires can be obtained depending on size of the gaps and combinations of dry, not so dry, and damp logs and their size. More or less light, bigger or smaller flame, quicker or slower burn down can be obtained by slightly moving the logs within the bonfire.

Simple "Eye" Survey of the Field Study Site

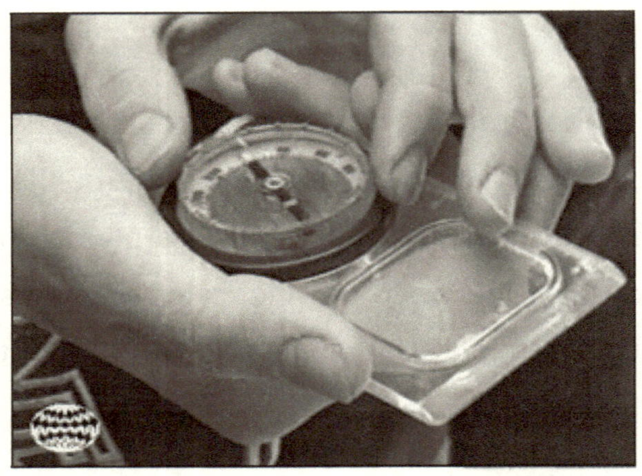

This manual describes a procedure for creating a simple "eye" survey of a field study site leading to a large-scale map of the study area. It contains several different techniques of complex surveying including: field sketching, a method of detour, polar method, a method of intersections and a method of perpendiculars.

Introduction

Conducting ecological field studies creates the need to plot observed objects, phenomena and sites on a map. That, in turn, entails mastering skills of correct map-and plan making and their proper usage.

The simplest methods of field site survey are usually applied in the course of ecological studies; they do not require special equipment or precise instruments. Such studies usually involve **large-scale** surveying, i.e. survey of small field sites with high detail.

A draft, where a horizontal projection of a small site is taken as being flat and plotted in a reduced and similar form is called a *plan*.

A draft, where a large site or the whole area is plotted taking into consideration its **general contour or relief,** is called a *map*.

A survey that allows a person to make a plan or a map without taking into account relief and crookedness of the surface is called *plane survey*.

A survey that allows the study of heights of certain sites is called *vertical surveying* or leveling.

Students will master the simplest skills of plane surveying with the help of only a compass and by counting steps at the given practical part of the lesson. They will not require any other equipment or instruments except a tape measure and a stable flat surface.

Introductory part of the lesson

The lesson should begin with some instruction: students should review concepts of a plan, a map, scale and conventions, which have been learned earlier in the lesson devoted to orienteering (Lesson #1, fall).

The introductory or theoretical part of the lesson should contain an explanation of **techniques** for eye surveying an area – making a field sketch, a method of detour, a polar method, method of intersections and a method of perpendiculars. The subsequent fieldwork will likely include all or some the above-mentioned techniques depending on the structure of the area and objects for surveying. Each of the techniques is described below in corresponding chapters.

Students should again master the **practical skills** of angles (azimuths) measurement (reminder: an azimuth is an angle between the direction to the North and the direction to the desired object, which is measured clockwise) as well as skills of distance measurement by counting steps (see Lesson #1, Autumn).

Structure of the field studies

Objectives of the present practical lesson include **making a plan** of the site in the immediate vicinity of the school or ecological field study center, onto which the main landmarks are plotted: forest tracks, water-bodies, roads, paths, forest cuttings, buildings, power transmission lines, etc. The size of the site for surveying depends on the number of students who accomplish the task and the structure of the site, i.e. the "simplicity" of the given area.

Students usually **work in groups** of 10-12 people in the Ecological Field Study Center "Ecosystem," which is located in a forest massif. They make a survey of part of a forest site that measures 500 m x 500 m. At the same time, a group of the same number of students conducts a survey of another site, located in the river floodplain, with a size of only 50 m x 100 m. It is obvious that the time spent on surveying depends on the number of details that have to be plotted on a map. There are only two glades, one path and four forest cuttings along the perimeter of the forest site, whereas a small site in the floodplain contains a meandering shoreline, a stream, several paths, a lake, a slope of the terrace located above the floodplain, etc. In other words, the teacher determines the size of the site for surveying according to the complexity of the task.

The number of students who work together also depends on the structure of the site. When surveying a complex site, for example, a river floodplain, it is optimal to divide the group into teams of 3-4 students. Each team should be given a certain site for surveying so that the surveyed sites can be combined into one general plan of the area at the closing part of the lesson.

When surveying a simple but vast site, for instance, a rectangular forest massif, it is advised to divide the group into smaller teams of two students and each of them is sent to the forest massif along parallel routes so that a combined plan of the forest site will be made at the end of the lesson.

It is advised to spend at least one hour on a **training survey** prior to independent fieldwork. To accomplish this training, the whole group should be divided into teams and all teams led simultaneously (next to each other, for instance, at an interval of 10 meters) along the same route (for example, along a closed polygon). Each team conducts an eye survey along the route independently, i.e. it draws a field sketch, measures angles and distances. Then the teacher checks whether teams fulfill all the procedures correctly. The given stage of the lesson is aimed at **training students** in practical skills, giving consultations and instructions in difficult situations and checking for correct results. Finally, it is necessary to make sure that all students are comfortable with survey techniques and can work independently.

The main part of field study is an independent **eye survey of a site**, making a field sketch, and measurements of angles and distances.

As eye survey of a site is a combination of different surveying techniques; we provide a description of all of them below.

Making a field sketch

A field sketch is an important part of map-making. A researcher in the field usually draws it freehand. The aim of sketch making is **methodical**. It is much easier to draw a plan after a sketch of an area has been drawn in the field; it is also possible to plot results of measurements, angles (azimuths) and distances of main objects and directions.

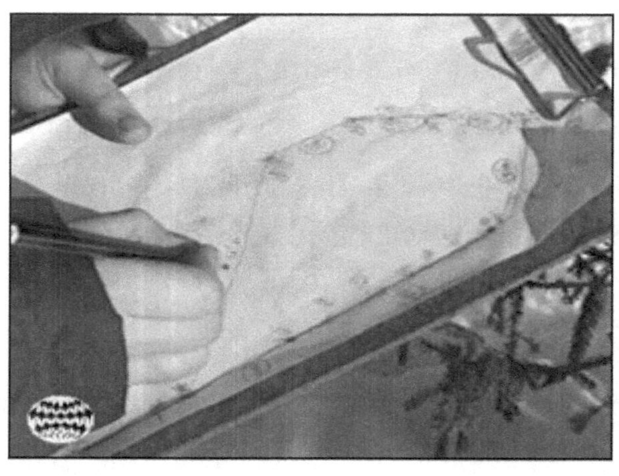

It is more convenient to draw a field sketch in pencil on a square piece of paper fixed on a flat surface. If it rains and the sketch gets soaked, the measuring data can be written down into a field notebook. In either case, whether data of measurements is recorded in the field log or plotted on the drawing, it is necessary to make notes as accurate as possible – so that when making a plan in the laboratory one will not get confused by the data.

Techniques for eye survey

All the diversity of positional relationship of points can be covered by **several techniques** that are used according to the peculiarities of the area under study. All techniques for survey are based on geometric rules and produce the necessary results for finding a positional relationship of points on the earth's surface.

A method of detour (changing directions)

This technique is applied when measuring *contours, borders, roads* and other more or less *straight sites*. It is also the main method in conduction of eye survey.

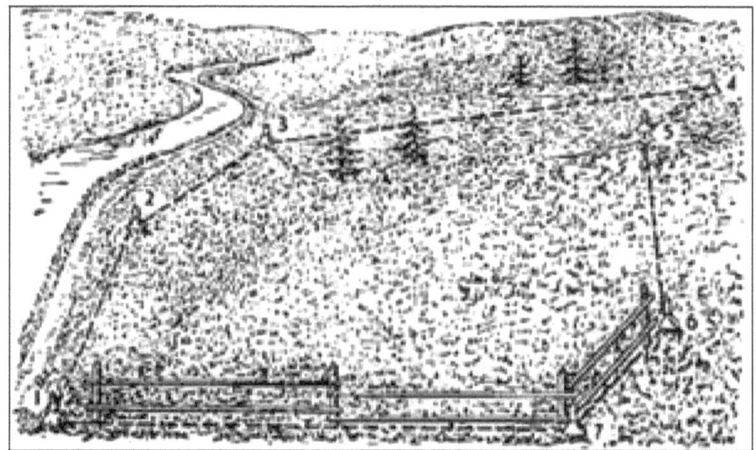

When carrying out a survey according to the **method of detour**, the beginning and the end of straight sites (lines of roads, forest cuttings, etc.) are marked with points, then distances between points are measured, angles (azimuths) of all the main landmarks and the course lines are measured at points.

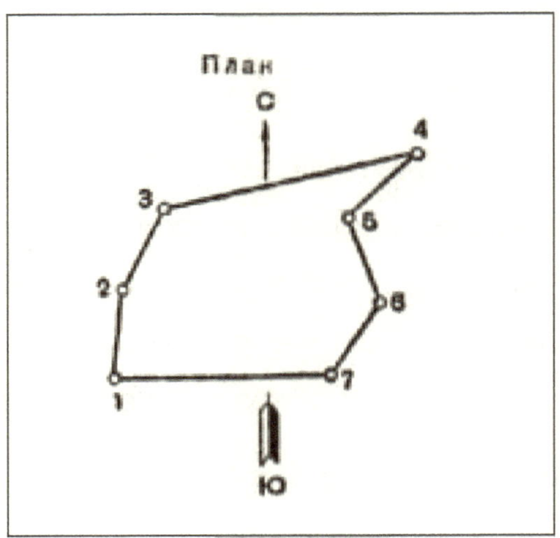

Measurements according to the method of detour result in a closed polygon with known angles and sides, so that it is possible to draw a contour of the future site.

The method of detour is **an initial stage** of surveying of any closed site, for instance a forest massif, if it has a polygonal shape.

A polar method (comparisons to magnetic north)

This technique is applied to a survey of *open sites* limited by curved contours (yards, glades in the forest, etc.) and consists of the following: First, a main (zero) point is chosen anywhere within the site, for example, in its center. Then angles (azimuths) of all visible landmarks which are well-seen and important for plan-making are measured with the help of a compass in the zero point – points A, B, C and D.

The next step is the measurement of distances between the zero point (0) and all the landmarks by counting steps or with the help of a tape measure.

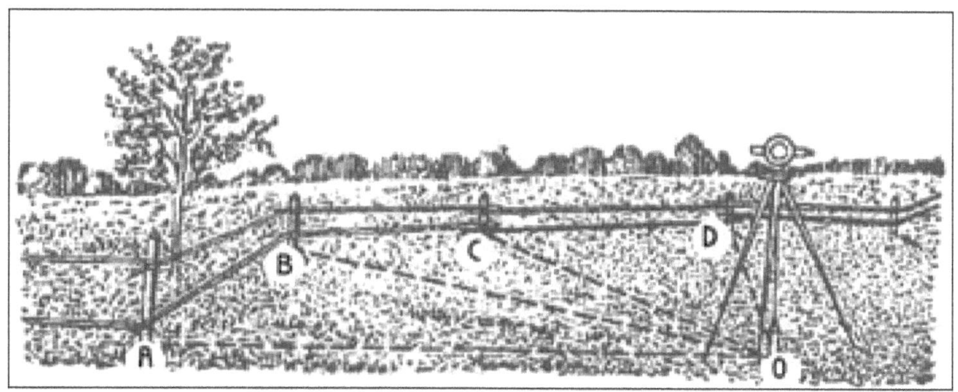

Use of the described method provides an opportunity to divide the whole area under study into sectors or triangles, where angles between radii and length of the radii are measured.

When plotting the data of the described survey, triangles OAB, OAC and others are plotted side by side based on two sides and an angle between them, so it results in a drawing of a similar figure on paper.

Method of intersections

This method is based on a geometric rule that in order to solve a **triangle** it is necessary to find length of only one side and the values of adjoining angles.

This technique is applied when the positional relationship of two points is known beforehand and it is necessary to find the location of the third point according to those points.

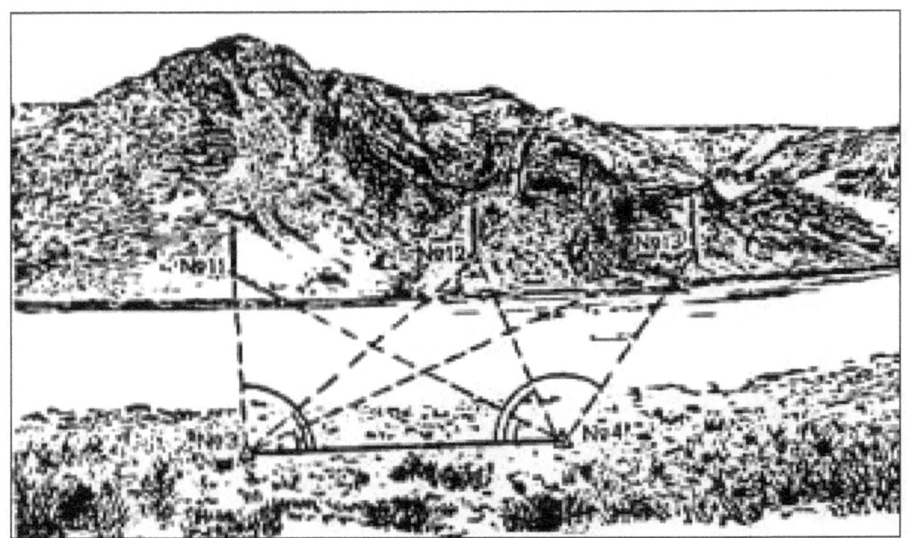

The method of intersections is applied to finding **remote points**, as well as to determination of points that are inaccessible for direct measurement (situated on the other bank of a river, a ravine, etc.)

Method of perpendiculars

This method consists in the following: the location of certain points in the area are determined in relation to an **auxiliary line** – the main – with the help of perpendiculars which are directly measured.

For instance, to survey a river, two straight lines are situated along the river. The most protruding points are measured on the riverbank and they are determined from the main lines with the help of perpendiculars.

Distances along the main lines to bases of perpendiculars are taken down in the course of line measuring. All figures are provided with descriptions in the field sketch as it is shown in the picture.

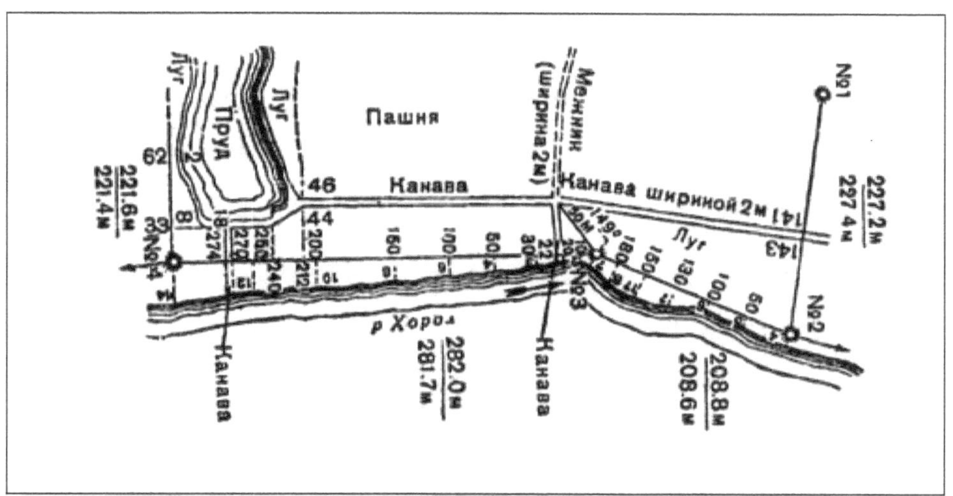

This technique is often applied to surveys of **elongated curved** and **broken contours** (for instance a river shoreline); the main lines are plotted along the contours and distances from them to characteristic points on contours are measured.

Distance measurement

Measurement of small distances (up to 50 meters) can be done with the help of a tape measure (linen tape measure in a bobbin, which is 10, 20 and 50 m long, can be bought in a building materials store).

When surveying vast sites (more than 100 m in diameter) it is better to apply a method of step counting (the procedure of how to teach students to measure distances by counting steps is described in the manual for Lesson #1, fall), although it is not as precise.

Eye survey of the site

While conducting ecological field studies it is often necessary to **quickly** obtain a **rough plan** of a certain site as a basis for plotting a number of special geographical or biological objects on it.

If a plan of the site is not available or if an available plan does not represent the facts, then the **complex eye survey** can be conducted successfully. It allows students to get a rather reliable though quite approximate representation of the site with the help of eye survey.

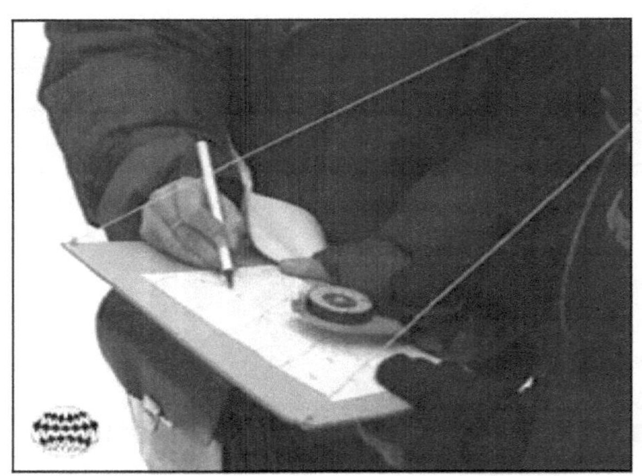

It is necessary to have a field notebook with a hard cover or a *plywood board* with a flat surface, paper for a sketch, a small right triangle with millimeter points and a compass (a liquid one is preferable) on a transparent board-ruler (for orienteering). The compass is fixed in the corner of the notebook or a flat surface and serves for orientation of the sketch in relation to the North and South.

Eye survey can be a **route** one – i.e. for surveying of a direction or a narrow strip of land (20-50 meters to both sides of the route), for instance, a road, a river, a border, etc. and a **complete** one, which is applied when surveying a limited site.

When conducting an eye survey it is necessary to pay special attention to the orientation of the flat surface at the point where the survey is conducted. To orient a flat surface means to hold it horizontally in front of you so that a magnetic needle of the compass and the direction of the line the North and South, which has been plotted on the field sketch, are parallel. After the flat surface has been oriented, you can proceed with the survey itself.

First, a **"point 1"** should be plotted on the plane-table, which corresponds with a point of standing on the ground so that the desired field sketch or its certain part will be put in the plane-table with the given orientation according to a chosen scale of survey. Then sightings (directions) from the initial point to all the outstanding landmarks (posts, trees and detached buildings, cross-roads, hills, etc.) are plotted on the oriented sketch on the flat surface with the help of a triangle. All the directions should be clearly drawn in a thin line in pencil. Then angles of each of the landmarks to be measured are written down directly on the outline or in the table of the field notebook. Thus, a **polar method** of surveying is used in the standing point.

The direction to point 2, which lies ahead and is assigned as the next point, should be measured precisely and accurately.

Then one should start to move to the determined point (a technique of **detour** is applied), i.e. by counting steps and drawing all interesting peculiarities of the area under study (road forks, landmarks, etc.) for the purposes of the given survey. So a method of **intersections** is used in the course of surveying. When drawing all the details, distances should be eye measured and plotted on the sketch according to chosen scale.

When students come to the planned point 2 (the method of detour continues), the plane-table is again oriented according to the compass; an approximate length of the line between the initial and the second points is laid off according to scale and a number of counted steps, then the second point is marked. Then all desired landmarks ahead and on both sides as well as the points, which have been sighted before from the first point, are taken again (the **polar** method). Consequently, angles (azimuths) of the third point (ahead) and the first one (back) as well as of all the important objects are measured. Angles and distances between the first and the second points are written down on the field sketch or put into a table.

In order not to get confused in measurement data where there is distance data as well as angles, it is advised to mark angles with a symbol "°" and distances with an abbreviation "PS" (pair of steps).

It is clear that **three main methods** are used in the course of eye survey, the method of detour (in order to conduct a survey of the contour), the polar method (for the survey from the standing points) and the method of intersections (for the survey of remote objects along the survey line).

Along with the described methods, the method of perpendiculars can also be used for plotting curved and elongated contours along the survey line. Thus, all four methods are used in eye survey; their application depends on peculiarities of the area under study.

When surveying a large area, it is necessary to follow a survey of borders and make a sketch of the site contour by the survey of details within the site. This is done by laying additional paths and plotting them on the general sketch. The survey within the site is conducted mainly by moving along straight lines and measuring distances between main linear objects (crossing of the line with paths, roads, water-courses and borders) and measuring angles of all the obvious landmarks (a polar method). Such paths should start and end at points, which are already present on the sketch and correspond with certain points in the site.

It is useful to show the **direction** of river current, streams, and slopes of relief with the help of small arrows on the sketch simultaneously with eye survey.

Careful eye survey will provide a rather pictorial and reliable drawing, which can be used as a basis for other ecological studies.

Processing the measuring data and plan-making

When coming back to the field center, a plan of the area is made on the basis of the field sketch drawn by hand with all plotted **angles** (azimuths) and **distances** (or notes in field notebook) according to a chosen scale.

The scale should be chosen so that the site that has been measured in the field will fit a sheet of a standard size and there will be enough space left for the title and conventions.

First, all distances which have been measured by **step-counting** should be calculated in meters – the notes should be written down

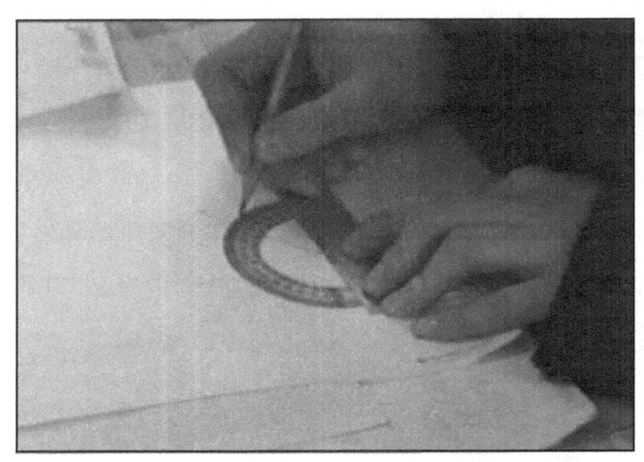

directly on the field sketch or in the working table (a calculator is needed).

The sketch is then transferred on to a clear sheet with the help of a ruler and a protractor (a round protractor is preferable). It is transferred in the same order as the field sketch has been drawn. All distances should be laid off according to the chosen scale, and all angles are drawn with the help of a protractor. Angles (azimuths) are measured from the vertical of the sheet, by superposing the zero point of the protractor with conventional direction to the North at the plan (usually the North is located at the top of the map or a plan). It is more convenient to plot the drawing on a graph paper from this point of view.

In most cases, the end of the last section of survey does not fall into the initial (starting) point and we come to a **discrepancy** of the survey. The distance between the initial and the end points obtained on the drawing (which is calculated according to the scale) will denote **absolute discrepancy**. The quotient of division of absolute discrepancy, for instance, 20 m by a length of the survey route, for instance, 2.4 km, i.e. 1:120 is called a **relative discrepancy** and it gives an idea about the accuracy and reliability of the conducted survey.

The maximum allowable relative discrepancy for eye survey should not exceed 1:50. If the relative discrepancy is much smaller than the given value 1:50 (1:300, 1:200) then the drawing can be left without changes, however if the discrepancy is considerable, but still less than 1:50, then the plan should be corrected by shifting of all the points except the first one in the direction of the discrepancy (from the starting point to the final one) for the values which are proportional to the absolute discrepancy and the distance between the shifting vertex and the initial point. That means that the farther the point is from the starting point, the farther it should be moved, thus, the final point should be moved for a distance equal to the whole discrepancy and will coincide with the initial point.

It is obvious that if the positions of the main points on the plan should be changed then it is necessary to correct the positions of all the other points that have been determined from the mentioned points (with the help of the method of intersections, the polar method and the method of perpendiculars).

When all the objects and landmarks are plotted on the plan and the discrepancy is corrected, the plan should be finalized – i.e. it is necessary to draw a **frame** (along the perimeter of the sheet), then the **title** should be written at the top of the sheet within the frame (for instance, "Plan of the site in the vicinity of …"). All names of objects and landmarks should be written on the plan and they should be marked with **conventions**. Conventions are drawn and described at the bottom of the sheet within the frame. The **scale** of the plan and **names of the plan authors** should also be written down at the bottom.

Study of growth dynamics of trees based on annual rings

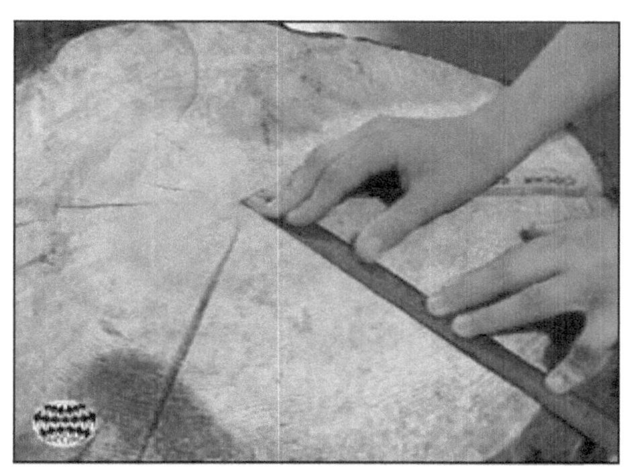

This manual describes an elementary procedure for the preparation of a tree trunk cross-section and subsequent counting of annual growth rings. The information will then be used to sketch a graph of the dynamics of tree growth in years and further analyze the tree growth in connection with changes in environmental factors.

Introduction

The given educational task is devoted to the determination of the **age** of a tree based on the number of annual rings and the study of peculiarities of tree **growth** during various years based on the width of these rings.

The annual rings seen in a cross-section cutting of a tree trunk of a tree grown in a moderate climatic zone occur as a result of the varying rates of growth during a vegetative season. The cells that are formed in the spring and summer have a lighter tone. The cells that are formed at the end of the vegetative season form wood that is composed of smaller cells whose cell walls are thicker than the ones formed in the spring and summer. The color of these smaller cells is darker than those formed in the beginning of the summer. Thus, an annual ring has light and dark components, and as a result, we can see borders of annual rings on the cut cross-section of the tree.

This occurs only in those zones of the earth where there is a noticeable change of seasons. In regions without a change of seasons, for example on the equator, annual rings are also formed, but they are practically invisible - wood has a even coloring.

By looking at the number of annual rings on the cut cross-section of a trunk it is possible quite **accurately to define the age of the tree**. The width of one annual ring, i.e. annual growth ring, varies from one year to the next. The width depends on tree state (condition) during the given vegetative season, which, in turn, depends on annual climatic peculiarities (features), health of the tree and many other factors.

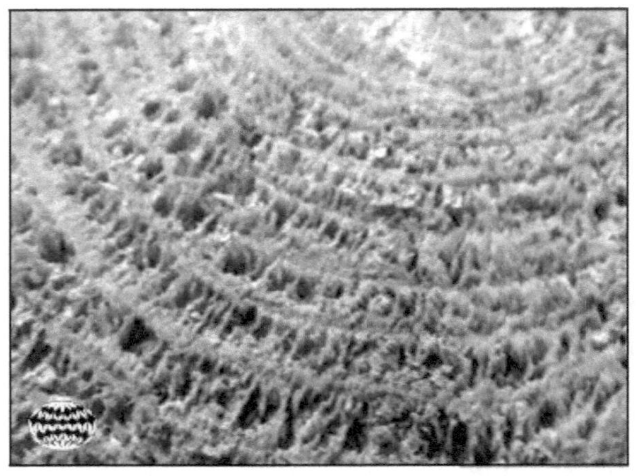

The average width of rings of different tree species varies and is basically associated with the species, the place it is grown, and individual features of the given tree. However, there are some typical features for all tree species or for the majority of trees of the same species. For example, rings are wider on the well-illuminated side of the tree than on the side of the tree that is in the shadow, therefore the stumps that remain from lone standing (grown) trees are used for the determination of Cardinal points (where North and the South are). Within a species beginning to grow under the forest canopy (in our woods they are, for example, spruce and oak) it is possible to observe objective changes of ring width during the first years of the trees life: while the young tree is growing in the shade, rings are narrow, when it begins getting more sunlight, rings become wider.

Natural loss (fallout) and the cutting of neighboring trees during forest management (maintenance) can also influence the width of the rings. When a "window" (opening) is formed near a growing tree, it begins to actively grow, growing both in height and in thickness.

The goal of this lesson is the preparation of a tree cross-section and the construction of a graph of its growth. Interesting results can be determined if students prepare cross-sections of several trees, growing in one general area but under different environmental conditions (for example different habitats) and then comparing the graphs.

We recommend doing this laboratory-based activity as part of winter ecological field studies during cold weather, while other outdoor field studies may be difficult and uncomfortable to execute.

For this lesson it is **necessary to have**: two-handled saw and metal ruler. For preparation of a permanent cross-section for multiple years, it is necessary to have a metal strip and nails.

Preparation of the cut cross-section

The study of growth dynamics of a tree can be conducted at any time of year and without dependence on weather conditions. For conducting the study, a saw, a ruler, a pen, in some cases a magnifying glass and some painting substance such as bluing or potassium permanganate are required (if no prepared cross-sections are available).

A wind-fallen tree or a standing dead tree should be found in the forest, whose year of dying off can be defined. If the needles still remain on a tree, then the current year can be taken for the year that it died. If there are no needles, but the smallest branches are present – the tree died the previous year. If there are no needles and there are no small-sized branches present, but the cortex is well preserved – it died about two years ago. It is advisable not to use older trees as

it is impossible to define the year of the tree's death precisely, so all further attempts will produce no results due to absence of the "starting point" of chronological scale.

An ideal tree for the preparation of cut cross-section is **a recently wind fallen tree**. Its death is not caused by natural reasons, i.e. by illnesses or pests, but by the influence of external forces. The analysis of such trees gives good results on the growth dynamics of the tree during its last years.

Cut the cross-section of the trunk as close to the base of the tree as possible. This is recommended for a more accurate estimation of the year of tree's birth. In any case, at the subsequent estimation of the year of tree's birth, a number of years are added to the calculated age of a trunk at the level of cutting. This number corresponds to the years that the tree has grown up to the height of cutting. Half a meter distance corresponds approximately to 5-7 years, about one meter, 10-12. The cut cross-section is made with a hand-held or power saw.

In order to cut an educational cross-section (i.e. not to be used only once but to be stored and subsequently examined many times by students), a disk is prepared, i.e. the trunk is twice sawed. Thus two cross-sections are made at the distance approximately about 10-15 cm from each other. A thinner disk may break apart, whereas a thick one will be too heavy. The disk is stripped in the lab. If the rings are not easily visible, it is possible to **dye** the cross-section, for example, with potassium permanganate, which will make the rings more distinct. For long-term storage and multiple use it is better to **frame** the edge of the disk along the circle with metal tape – it will protect the disk from breaking up when it dries and cracks (which is inevitable).

Estimations of ring width

The most responsible procedure for estimating the width of annual rings is done in the following order:

First, **a line** is sketched with a thin pencil; all measurements will be conducted along this line. The line should pass precisely from the

cross-section center to its external edge (along the radius). A sector of the trunk with the least number of anomalies - cracks, not concentric compressions, remains of knags, old leaked wounds etc. should be chosen for measurements. The line of measurements should cross the most "average" sector of wood.

Then a ruler with very distinct millimeter divisions (a metal ruler, for example) is applied to the external edge of last (outside) ring. The zero of the ruler should coincide with the external edge of the last ring. In order to make sure that the ruler cannot be shifted inadvertently while measuring, it is better to press it down with something heavy or to attach it to the wood with pins in several places.

A working table is then prepared for data recording of measurements (example):

Year	Mark	Growth	Year	Mark	Growth	Year	Mark	Growth
1999	0	2.2	1934	154.5	2.7	1878	344.5	5.2
1998	2.2	1.9	1933	157.2	1.8	1877	349.5	5.0

1997	4.1	...	1932	159.0	...	1876	354.5	...
...	...	...	...	...	...	...	...	...

The number of cells in the table should approximately correspond to age of the tree.

In the column "year," all years are recorded in advance, starting with the year of the tree's death, into the course of time, **back to the year of the tree's birth**, which is precisely defined when the measurements are over.

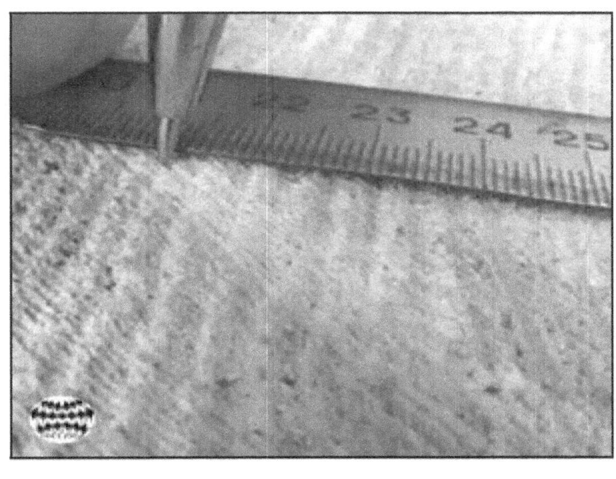

In the column "mark," readings of the position (location) of the next annual ring's **border** on the ruler are recorded in millimeters. Such measurements are taken consequently from the latest (external) to the very first annual ring (in the center of the cross-section), gradually moving from the cross-section edge to the center and recording each of the following measurements in the appropriate space of the table. Having added 5-10 years (depending on the height the cut was made) to the first year (in the center), the year of the tree's birth can be determined. This value has no principal importance; it can be approximate because the years are counted in the reverse order, starting with the last annual ring, which corresponds to a known year.

After completing the measurement of the rings' position along the radius (after filling in the "mark" column), **calculations of annual growth** should be recorded. They are calculated with the help of a calculator, subtracting the value of each older ring from the value of younger ring's disposition. For example, for the case indicated in the table – the value of 1998 (2.2) is deducted from the value of 1997 (4.1) and we determine annual growth in 1998 as equal to 1.9 mm. Such estimations are calculated for all years of the given cross-section. The data forms the **basis** for making a graph of the growth dynamics of the tree in years.

Graph plotting

On the basis of the data on annual growth the graph of dynamics of the tree's growth is plotted according to years. It is more convenient to plot it on squared or, even better - on scale paper.

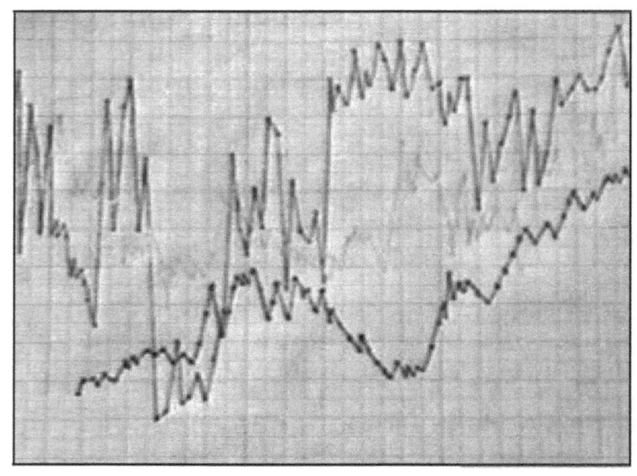

Years - from left to right starting with the year of the tree's birth to the last year of its life are laid off as abscissas. The years should not be plotted all in a row, because the marks would be too crowded together. Rather, place their marks on an axis of abscissas, one for each 10 years.

Absolute values of annual growth are laid off on the axis of ordinates in millimeters.

The scale should be chosen so that the axis of abscissas is approximately twice longer than the axis of ordinates. Then the graph will be visual and easily readable.

Data interpretation

Analyzing the graph, students should try to define years with **minimum** and **maximum** annual growth, and if possible, to discern **long periods** of the slowed and accelerated growth of the tree. It is necessary to try to connect these declines and rises with some external factors. It is ideal, if possible, to get data on climatic conditions of those years of abnormal growth. Such data is available at meteorological stations. Using their data it is possible to reveal those climatic factors, and to determine which factors had the greatest influence on the growth of trees.

When analyzing the graph, special attention should be paid to the **first and last years** in the life of the tree, as some interesting details can come to light whether the tree lived the first years in favorable conditions or how long it was sick before dying off (if the death was from natural causes). It is also interesting to analyze the influence of sanitary cutting and forest management cuttings on the growth of the tree in the past. For this purpose, it is possible to use the data on cuttings conducted by the local forestry station.

The work will be more interesting if several cut cross-sections are made of trees of different species or grown in different places (if sufficient "labor resources" are available). For example, it is possible to compare the dynamics of tree growth of a spruce and a pine, or pines from a pine forest, a mixed forest, and a swamp. In such cases common (general) regularities of a tree's growth in the region (we shall say which are determined by the climate) and individual features of trees (for example, vital status) are revealed.

The final report on the conducted study should consist of the graph of dynamics of tree growth (or several trees on the same graph) with revealed **periods** of slowed and accelerated growth. The **photos** and **explanatory description** (note) in the text should be attached to the graph, explaining observed facts and regularities (if found).

Mapping forest vegetation

This manual describes two procedures for vegetation mapping: complete and transect mapping. The stages of field studies are described including reconnaissance survey, determination and mapping of plant associations and geobotanical description of typical vegetation. Related lab studies include mapping and analysis of the spatial distribution of vegetation.

Introduction

The study of ecological interrelationships of any area should result in the determination of **spatial distribution** patterns for components of the ecosystems at the given area, mainly — revealing interrelationships between the vegetation and its biotope.

As mentioned above, such data can be obtained by two major procedures: by establishing and describing an integrated landscape profile, and by geobotanical map-making. Procedures for establishing and describing the profile were discussed in previous lessons in the autumn field studies course. In this lesson students will learn how to make a **geobotanical map**.

Methods and results of vegetation studies by making profiles and by map-making are similar, though each procedure has its own peculiarities and objectives.

Results of profiling are shown visually in the form of the profile drawing – a vertical "section" of the site under study (**a side view**), whereas results of geobotanical map-making are expressed in the form of a colorful map (**an "aerial" view**).

Vegetation studies resulting in a profile can better demonstrate vegetation changes depending **on relief** (for instance, along the line "valley-watershed"), whereas a geobotanical map can better illustrate **contours** of plant associations, their diversity and the correlation of different plant associations.

A secondary goal – why we study vegetation – has influence upon the selection of the method of vegetation representation. When studying vegetative cover, it is advised to study it by making **a profile** as it can better show peculiarities of vegetation distribution and its connection with relief and soils. A complex profile is suggested when conducting an integrated ecological or special geobotanical study.

When conducting monitoring and zoological investigations, for instance, when studying pollution or ionizing radiation background, or when studying the nesting areas of birds or structure of mammal populations, it is recommended to study vegetation by **a map-making method**. It is advised to make geobotanical maps when studying other objects if their distributions depend on vegetation (invertebrates, lichens, fungi, etc.)

Procedures for vegetation mapping

Geobotanical maps as well as other maps are divided according to scale into small-, middle- and large-scale maps. This lesson will focus on making large-scale geobotanical maps without discussing the peculiarities of the world's vegetation and regions or botanical-geographical regions.

A **large-scale geobotanical map** gives one an idea about the distribution of plant associations on a limited site of the area under study; it indicates the nature of boundaries and changes among them.

A geobotanical map can be made in compliance with different procedures, starting from a complete geobotanical survey and ending with air or space mapping, however, we will limit our procedure to two variables for the purposes of the present lesson – complete mapping of a forest tract with the help of an eye survey method and mapping of a linear transect.

Which procedure should be given preference, depends first of all upon peculiarities of vegetation of the area under study.

1) It is advisable to apply a method of **complete mapping** at scale 1:5000 (50 m in 1 cm) in forested areas with **slightly disturbed** vegetative cover and more or less distinct changes in plant associations. The site can have an approximate size of 0.5 X 0.5 km (0.25 km^2).

2) It is recommended to use a procedure of **linear transects** to study sites with much **patchiness** of vegetative cover (parks, forest

belts) and in case there is no map-basis available. A linear transect is a belt of 70-100 meters wide and about 1 km long.

Complete mapping of a forest tract by an eye survey method

Complete mapping by an eye survey method involves walking the mapped site (it is a forest track, as a rule) along **a network of parallel routes** with simultaneous plotting of plant association boundaries on a ready cartographic framework with subsequent extrapolation of their contours for sections between routes.

Routes are laid down in straight lines parallel to each other at a distance of 50-100 meters from each other, depending on the complexity and patchiness of vegetation cover in forested areas or very rugged terrains.

While forest mapping, a group of students is divided into **teams** of 2 pupils. One team is given the task to map the forest track along the perimeter, whereas all other teams are sent into the heart of the forested area along parallel routes. Movement of groups within the forest site should be achieved strictly according to the compass. Researchers' objectives include step-counting and plotting all encountered boundaries of forest types on a draft map (the group of students, which moves along the perimeter should plot boundaries that go into the heart of the forest, whereas teams which map the forest track should plot boundaries of forest types which cross their route. Thus one member of the team only routes (goes strictly along the prescribed direction) and counts his or her steps, whereas the other member of the team watches changes in vegetation and plots boundaries of plant associations on a map.

The task becomes easier at a **non-forested or sparsely forested** (well-looked through) site with many landmarks – the survey is carried out by a method of "**detour**" (see Lesson #2 – Eye Survey of an Area). It is the simplest type of eye survey, where a survey route goes along a perimeter of plotted site or along boundaries between forest types and all the contours are plotted on a map by direct boundary tracking in the field.

Procedure for mapping at linear transect

This procedure is used at sites with a high degree of **patchiness** of vegetation cover or when a map of the area is not available. The

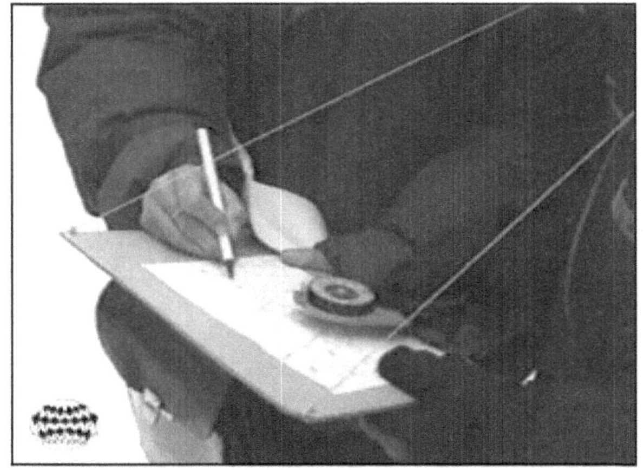

procedure is based on a procedure for transect (along a band) studies, which is diverse in zoological and zoogeographical features.

First **a route (transect)** on which mapping will be

conducted, is chosen for the transect studies. In practice, the transect is laid down on both sides of a narrow forest cutting, a road, power transmission lines, etc. Geobotanical mapping is carried out at belts of a specific width on both sides from the central line-guiding line.

The width of a belt for mapping can be chosen arbitrarily depending on the physical and technical abilities of students. The usual width of the belt is 30-50 meters on both sides off the central line.

The length of a transect also depends on the objectives and abilities of the researchers, and it usually amounts to 1.5 km.

There are **several stages** in transect mapping:

The first stage is **reconnaissance mapping**. It is conducted in order to give a general idea of the structure of vegetation at the chosen site and detection of plant association contours. In fact, this stage replaces making a foundation map in the case of complete mapping of a forest area.

Reconnaissance mapping is usually carried out by 3-5 groups of students. One group moves along the transect centerline (along a road, a forest cutting), and 2-4 other teams move along parallel routes depending on visibility range from the centerline. Each team draws "contour" – a hand-written sketch of the area independently. Students plot all landmarks and approximate boundaries of plant associations in crossover points with the transect.

The second stage is **marking plant association boundaries**. White sheets of paper can serve as markers; they should be fixed to tree trunks or pinned on poles that are stuck into the ground (it is better to pin them on branches and poles, as markers will be well-seen not only from the centerline, but also from other points in the heart of the forest belt.)

Distances between plant association boundaries are measured in the course of the third stage, then boundaries are **plotted on a scheme** of a transect according to a chosen scale.

Using a tape measure, it is possible to obtain accurate data of distance measurements. However, it requires much time, and moreover, it is almost impossible to use a tape measure in dense underbrush and undergrowth. Distances can be easily and quickly measured by step-counting (the length of the leader's step should be accurately measured).

The final stage is the determination of plant association boundaries **in the heart** of the forest belt under study.

Geobotanical descriptions when vegetation mapping

Determining the boundaries of plant associations (i.e. determination of plant associations) and their **geobotanical description** according a standard procedure, is an integrated part of vegetation mapping. This procedure has already been used in the lesson entitled "Complex studies at a landscape profile" (autumn field study course).

Detection of vegetative patterns and their boundaries

Geobotanical surveys start with the determination of plant associations, which are found within the area under study. It is the most "intellectual" part of the work; students are required to have knowledge of not only certain plant species, but also to be familiar

with typical vegetation or, on the contrary, make a determination of only one plant association (for example, - forest). Determining the plant associations is quite subjective, especially for beginners. In order to make this initial stage of work easier for students, a teacher can show and "name" plant associations within studied area.

Let us repeat that when determining vegetative patterns and associations at a profile, it is important not to go "too deep" into identification of "micro-communities." Only major, "contrasting" plant associations, which are easily recognized visually along the profile line, should be determined.

Geobotanical descriptions of plant associations

In the case of complete mapping, geobotanical descriptions are made right along the route – at each change in vegetation type. In the case of transect mapping, the stage of geobotanical description can be done right after all boundaries have been plotted on the map (as there are markers along the transect line which indicate boundaries of vegetative patterns).

Geobotanical descriptions are carried out in each forest type. It is more convenient and correct to make descriptions at sites of 10 x 10 m or 20 x 20 m (depending on vegetation density). However, they can be made without laying sites – just in any other typical site of the given plant association.

The description is made according to a standard procedure using "Vegetation description form" (see sample at the end of the manual), i.e. a table is drawn with columns for each feature of vegetation description. Forms are filled in directly on site – where description is carried out.

Filling in a form cap

At first general information about the planned landscape/vegetation description and location of the test site (**date, authors**, and **number of the description**) is recorded on the form.

The **administrative and local position** - region, position in relation to the nearest human settlements - is further described. A local position – as detailed as possible - is described i.e. directions how to find the site of description. For example: *0.4 km to the North of..., on an eminence, near forest edge;* or *0.85 km along the road in the direction of the highway from..., near a large boulder.*

Position in relief – optional description of the site location, for example: *on a flat place; on a slope towards a stream or a gully; on a* *river terrace; in a depression, in a gully, on an eminence, hillock, on a riverbank, at the edge of a scarp etc.*

Environment - the characteristic features of the surrounding locality are described: *a swamp, a meadow, a field, any forest type, a river or stream bank, presence of a road or other anthropogenic object etc.*

Described area (m x m) is the size of the site where description is carried out. Usually sites of about 10 x 10 or 20 x 20 are chosen for description of forest associations, whereas sites with the size of 1m x1m are selected for the description of meadows.

Name of the plant association - The name of a plant community is formed of the names of dominant plant species (or ecological groups) from each layer of the phytocoenese. Thus the species within limits of the same layer are listed in **ascending order** of their total numbers.

The full name of forest vegetative structure includes four basic components of vegetative cover – a forest layer, a bush layer, a moss-lichen layer and an herbaceous-shrub layer.

They are listed in exactly the same order as described here, for example: *a birch-pine forest with underwood consisting of spruce, filbert-mountain ash, and pleutropous bilberry – small-reed.* It is a forest where pine and birch dominate <u>in the arboreal layer</u> (more pines, fewer birches), mountain ash and filbert dominate in <u>a bush layer</u> (mountain ashes prevail), a moss *Pleurozium schreberi* dominates in <u>a moss layer</u>, small-reed prevails in <u>the herbaceous-shrub layer</u> with less (or as much) of bilberry.

Sometimes, depending on the purpose of the description, a simplified name of the forest can be given, listing main ecological groups of plants, which form the phytocoenose, for example: *a birch-pine green moss-mixed herbaceous forest*. In this forest, pine and birch prevail in the arboreal layer; an ecological group of green mosses (various species) dominates in the moss-lichen cover, and cereals and meadow plants of rich soils – in the herbaceous-shrub cover.

The forests with developed moss-lichen cover are usually subdivided into three types corresponding to prevailing ecological plant groups of this layer: white-mosses (with a cover of lichens), long-mosses (with a cover of sphagnum and hair-cap mosses) and green-mosses (with a cover of *Pleurozium* and *Hylocomium* etc.).

It should be remembered that the name given by a researcher is rather conventional, thus it does not characterize the mentioned plant association in full. The name is given in order to make subsequent analysis easier, so it should not be too long.

The description of arboreal (tree) and bush layers

After filling in a cap of the form (general information on the biotope) the description of arboreal and bush layers follows. It includes a determination of crowns' density, formulas of the forest stand, diameters and heights of trunks, heights of crowns' attachment (lower crown's edge) and age of trees (see the example at the end of this manual).

For the purposes of the given educational task (a study of layered structure of the forest will be further discussed) parameters of crowns' density and formulas of forest stand should be estimated **separately** for each forest canopy: for adult forest stand, young growth and understory. It is determined by the practical convenience of such separation and relative simplicity of the procedure record-keeping for an abundance of arboreal and shrub plants.

Crown density

The description of a layer should start with an estimation of crown density.

Crown density is a portion of the ground surface area covered with crown projections. It can also be characterized as the part of the sky that is closed by crowns. In other words, the ratio between "open sky" and crowns should be estimated.

Density, abundance and other similar values in geobotany are usually evaluated with the help of one of the three parameters: percentage (from 0 up to 100), in numbers (points) (from 1 up to 10) and in fractions of a unit (from 0.1 up to 1), which is, in fact, the same.

Density of crowns is usually expressed fraction of a unit - from 0.1 up to 1, i.e. the absence of crowns is taken as zero, and complete closeness of crowns is 1. Thus, openings among branches are not taken into account; a "crown" is space outlined mentally along external branches (perimeter) of the crown.

In this connection, a dense birch forest (for example, in winter) may seem completely "transparent" looking upwards, but in fact, at closer examination it can appear to be of maximum density (closed) (up to 1). A good psychological method for the determination of deciduous forest density when there are no leaves on the trees is to imagine this forest in summer, at complete foliage. It helps students learn to quickly and correctly estimate crown density at any time of year.

After evaluating species composition and crown density of the arboreal (tree) layer, the same parameters should be estimated for **young growth and underwood**.

Young growth consists of young trees of the main forest-forming species of the given forest up to 1/3 high of the main canopy (ripe forest stand). Young growth is allocated as a *separate canopy of the arboreal (forest) layer*. **Underwood** consists of arboreal and bush species, which can never form a forest stand. Typical examples of young growth in a pine-spruce forest are young spruces, pines, and birches, whereas underwood consists of willows, mountain ashes, buckthorns, raspberry etc.

It is always a little bit more difficult to determine density of the young growth and underwood due to their small height and because it is not always possible "to look against the light" from below upwards.

Strictly speaking, there is another parameter for evaluation of the abundance (relative numbers) of herbaceous and shrub plants in geobotany - descriptive (projective) cover. It is expressed in percentages: less than 10 % - individual plant specimens, 100 % - complete density. Due to the similarity of parameters for crown density and projective cover, we recommend to use a parameter of crown density for both forest and shrub layers in the given educational task.

In order to learn how to use the procedure of crown density evaluation for young growth and underwood, a reverse psychological trick can be applied: density is estimated as a projection of crowns on the ground; in this case one should imagine, for example, what kind of shadow the crowns of low trees and bushes will produce and what percentage of the ground would be covered with this shadow.

Crown density should be estimated **separately** for each of the defined layers and canopies of the forest - ripe forest stand, young growth, and understory.

It is easier to learn how to estimate when imagining that there are no other layers and canopies in the forest except the one presently under study, and then trying to estimate the crown density of this very layer. Then it is necessary to proceed with each subsequent layer. It should be noted that in complex multi-layered forests, the total density of crowns of various layers could be more than 1 (due to overlapping of crowns in different layers).

Formula of the forest stand

After crown density is estimated, a formula of the forest stand should be composed. It is an estimate of the share (fraction) taken up by a separate species in arboreal and bush layers.

In forest geobotany a share of various trees is determined by a ration of trunks. The share of each species in the formula of the forest is usually expressed in points - from 1 up to 10. The total number of trunks of all plants is considered to be equal to 10, and then the estimations are calculated: what part (share) each separate species takes. If the representation of autonomous (separately growing) plants in the forest is less than 10 % (less than 1 point), they are marked in the formula with a "+" sign, whereas individual plants (1-2 specimens within the studied site) are marked with the sign "ind."

Names of species in the forest formula are reduced to one or two letters, for example: birch - B, oak - O, pine - P, spruce - S, aspen - As, speckled alder – SA, European alder - EA, linden - Ln, larch - La, buckthorn - Bt, raspberry – Rs, filbert – F, etc.

Examples of the formulas of the canopy of an adult forest stand:

1) The formula 6S4B means that the ripe forest stand is formed with 60% spruce and 40 % birch.

2) The formula 10S means that the forest is homogeneous, consisting of only one species - spruce.

3) The formula 10S+B means that in the forest stand there is a minor admixture of birches in the spruce forest.

Taking into account the importance of crown density evaluations as well as the formulas for each of the forest canopies, the records in the description form can, for example, look as follows:

Arboreal and bush layers	Crown density	Formula
Ripe forest stand	0.8	6S 2P 2B
Young growth	0.3	10S
Understory	0.1	5Bt 5 F + Rs

These records mean in the described forest there is a dense canopy of ripe trees. Eighty percent of the space in the top part of the forest is occupied with crowns. Thus, spruce prevails, fewer pines and birches are found, and in equal quantity to each other. There is a rather dense young growth of spruce (an intensive reforestation). Understory is thinned out and consists of buckthorn and filbert at approximately equal shares with separate sprinklings of raspberry.

Description of arboreal and bush layers also includes such important information about their structure as the diameter of trunks (D 1.3), height of the forest stand (Hfs), height of crown attachment (Hca) and age of plants.

The **diameter** (D) is measured for several tree trunks that are typical for the given forest at chest height (~1.3m), and then an average diameter is calculated. If necessary it is possible to mark minimum and maximum values for each canopy as well.

The measurements are taken either with a special tree caliper (large sliding calipers), or are based on the length of its circumference. For this purpose, the circumferences of all trees in the site are measured, and then an average value is calculated. The formula $D = c/\pi$, where D is diameter, c is circumference, and π is a constant, equals approximately 3.14 (in field conditions the length of a circle can be simply divided by three).

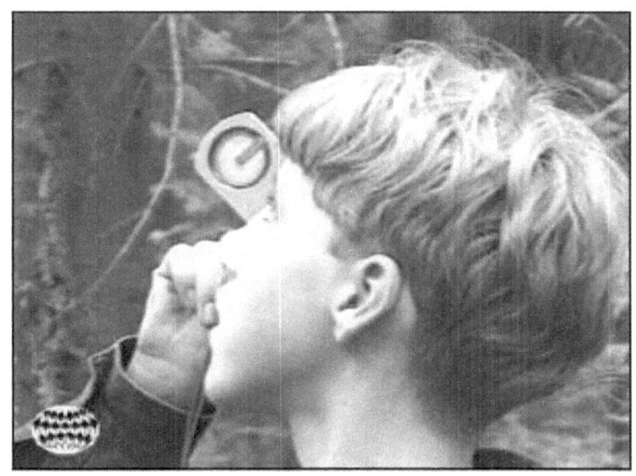

Height of the forest stand (Hfs) is an average height of trees in each separate layer. The measurement of height is carried out according to one of five methods: 1) using an **altimeter** – a special optical instrument, which measures a vertical angle at the object with subsequent estimation of the distance from the instrument to the base of the object (in this case, a tree), 2) **by eye** (which requires experience), 3) using a **tape measure** for measuring of one of the fallen trees of the given canopy, 4) the method of "counting people" and 5) the method of shadow measurement. The first three methods do not require any explanation.

The method of "**counting people**" consists of the following. Measurements are carried out by two people together: one person  stands close to the tree, and another, who is skilled at visual estimation, walks from the tree until he or she can cover the whole tree from the base up to the top in view. Then he or she tries to count how many people of the given height can be "stacked" along the trunk.

It is recommended each time to postpone distance, which is twice longer, than the previous one, i.e. while "moving" mentally along the tree trunk upwards, first, height of two "person" should be postponed, then height of two should be added, then – of four, then of eight etc. (i.e. according to the scheme: 1 - 2 - 4 - 8 -16). From the point of view of human visual estimation it is easier and more accurate. Knowing this "person's" height it is possible to calculate the height of the tree.

The fifth method is the most precise of all indirect methods, and is used in sunny weather. The **shadow** from a standing person whose height is known is measured precisely. The shadow from the studied tree is then also measured. In the dense forest, when the shadow of the given tree and, especially, its top is difficult to find, the following method can be employed. A person should walk from the tree so that his or her sight (head), the top of the tree, and the sun lie along one line. Then the person should find a shadow of his or her own head on the ground – which will also be a shadow of the top of the tree. Then only the distance between this point and the base of the tree should be measured. The height of the tree is estimated according to a proportion: length of the shadow of the person / its height - length of shadow of the tree / its height.

For the educational purposes it is possible to use a combination of several methods – so that measurements received by direct methods will verify results of measurements by indirect methods.

The **height of crown attachment** (H ca) is an average height at which lower living branches of trees are found (it is not recorded for the young growth or the understory).

Age of trees can be more reliably estimated according to the annual rings of cut trees, which can be found practically in any forest (of course it is not necessary to cut down trees for this purpose). Some recently cut trees or their stumps can be used for these purposes. If there no "fresh" stumps in the forest it is necessary to make a complete cut cross-section or to cut down a trunk of the fallen tree with an axe - at least up to its core. The cut cross-section should be taken out of the tree as close to its butt end as possible.

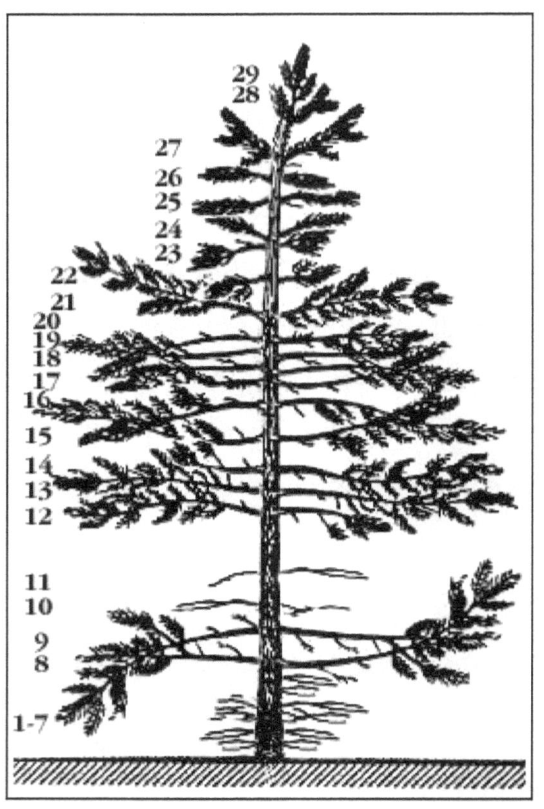

The age of the young growth is also defined according to annual rings using the example of one sawed or cut down plant (it is better to do this outside the studied site).

The age of young and middle-aged trees, spruces and pines in particular, can be defined according to whorls, which are several branches at the same level around the trunk along all its length. These plants still have dead (in the bottom part of a crown) or living (in the top part) branches, which grow by bundles – whorls -- until they are 30-40 years old (and sometimes even longer. The quantity of such whorls - from the base of the trunk up to its top, precisely corresponds to age of the tree, because during one vegetative season a tree grows one internode (one whorl). The number of years arrived at by counting whorls should be increased by at least three years, taking into account the rooting period and the start of growth.

A description of **grass-shrubby** and **moss-lichen** layers is not made in winter due to the presence of snow cover. If there is no snow, then students are limited to the determination of an approximate correlation of main plant species.

Let us repeat that the procedure for geobotanical descriptions with form-filling is carried out **for each of the found plant associations** on the whole area subject for mapping.

Making a geobotanical map

Boundaries and length of the revealed plant associations are plotted on the topographic map or on the transect line right in the field according to chosen scale.

In case of the transect method, it is more convenient to **mark vegetative patterns** on a map **with numbers**, and later in the lab, each separate biotope can be shown more vividly when finalizing the map (see below).

When eye survey mapping is over (especially along the transect line) it is advised to conduct one more **final passage** along the route in order to reveal and correct all inaccuracies and mistakes, which is especially important for those without much mapping experience (it often happens that after inexperienced "cartographers" get to know the area better in the course of description, boundaries of plant associations quite often "change their location!").

Laboratory processing of materials

Boundaries of detected plant associations should be plotted on an available map or made part of the plan of the transect in the result of field studies. Plant associations themselves should be marked with numbers and each number should correspond with one form of geobotanical description.

Descriptive forms are processed under laboratory conditions, and as the result of this work, a legend to the map is developed and the final map is drawn.

Making a legend of the geobotanical map

Making a legend is one of the most complicated and important parts of the laboratory work.

Any legend is made on the basis of vegetation **classifications**, which, in turn, take into account a set of **the most important characteristics** of plant associations.

However, the legend greatly differs from a classification scheme of vegetation. First of all, not all the taxons (units of classification) can be used in the legend, only the taxons, which **can be shown** according to the corresponding map-scale. Besides, if the classification is a system of subordinate units, then a legend allows one to show different taxonomical levels in different categories of vegetation and the totally different arrangement of taxons. Finally, not only the hierarchy of revealed units of the legend is taken into account, but also ecological, dynamic and other correlations.

While developing the legend, students should aim at not only taking into account the characteristics of vegetation itself, but also its **ecological and geographical connections.** When staring to make a legend, all found phytocenoses **are grouped according to vegetation types** (for instance, forests, meadows, swamps) and then other auxiliary taxons (formation, a group or class of formations) are defined if necessary within each vegetation type. Arrangement of taxons within the legend should begin with taxons belonging to the zonal type of vegetation.

It is desirable that the largest categories of the legend reflect **connection of vegetation with relief** in areas with diverse macro- and meso-relief form, where vegetation differs greatly.

Thus, it is possible to mark out separately vegetation of river-valley, large gullies and vegetation of placoric sites (watershed surface and section of the slope located near a watershed) in the legend. Then typological units of vegetation cover can be arranged within the limits of the legend subdivisions.

For instance, flood plain and continental meadows can be distinguished within the limits of a **meadow type of vegetation**, and then meadows of low flood plain and upper flood plain can be determined within flood-plain meadows, whereas lowland and dry meadows can be found among continental meadows. Plant associations within the site should be arranged according to the ecological principle- for example, in the order of increasing or decreasing moisture factor.

When representing **forest types** in the legend (especially in areas of long-term anthropogenic impact), their dynamics should also be shown by arranging all forest types according to degree of their disturbance (transformation series).

Aboriginal communities or **conventionally native** plant associations, which have undergone changes due to anthropogenic impact, although they managed to restore main characteristics of native communities, should be put on the first place. **Short-term secondary** plant associations, which differ in species composition from native associations, follow them but when anthropogenic impact is over, they can restore quickly and return to their initial state. **Long-term secondary communities**, i.e. heavily damaged forest types are placed at the end, when changes in forests affected not only vegetation, but also habitat conditions.

Presentation of mapping results

Field and laboratory studies result in a geobotanical map with **geobotanical sections** plotted on it, which are marked with colors, signs or combined **symbols**.

Vegetation features are indicated with the help of different **colors, tints, shading** and off-scale **symbols** when map-making.

Boundaries of plant associations are plotted along the whole area of the studied forest track or within the limits of mapped transect on the geobotanical map.

The color spectrum and numeration should correspond with the legend.

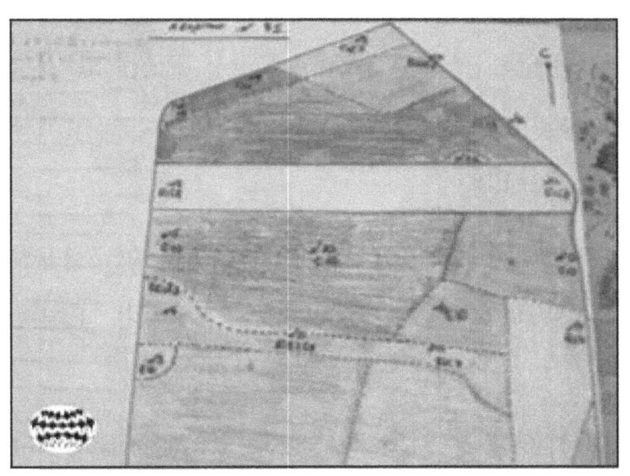

There are no strict **rules** for colorful design of large-scale maps. It is desirable that the color should more or less reflect main ecological conditions. For example, it is advised to use **warm colors** (pink, yellow) for representation of vegetation associated with drier habitats (dry meadows, vegetation found in sands, etc.), whereas **cool colors** (blue, violet, etc.) can correspond to wetter vegetation (swamps, valley meadows, etc.)

Brown tints are usually used for an indication of pine forests, whereas spruce forests are drawn in violet and deciduous forests, in different tints of green.

The color is usually given to a specific formation (pine, forest, spruce forest, small-leafed forest, etc.). Associations that are parts of the specific formation (spruce forest with presence of oxalis, spruce forest with dominance of green mosses, so on) are usually shown with the help of tints of the main color or shading against the main color. Shading is usually used when a plant formation contains many associations.

Vegetation dynamics is indicated on the map or a profile with the help of the following pictorial techniques: the native vegetation is painted in continuous color, whereas all derived communities are cored with bands or different tints of the main color used for the native vegetation. The heavier the community is transformed, the narrower the strip or the lighter the tint.

Besides the color, each association can additionally be given **conventional symbols** of dominating plant species for better visualization of the map.

Conventional symbols of plant species do not usually coordinate with the scale; however, it is necessary to take into account the relative size of plants and to use larger symbols for large plants and smaller symbols for smaller plants. It is recommended that conventional symbols more or less resemble appearance of the plant.

Conventional symbols make the map more visual; however, it is quite difficult to distinguish plant associations according to the symbols. That is why symbols should be used as an additional method of showing vegetation.

Analysis of plant community distribution patterns

The following statements should be clarified when analyzing distribution patterns of plant formations:

1) A brief description of botanical and geographical location of the area under study in zonal and regional divisions should be provided;

2) All factors which have the most influence upon specificity of plant formations and their spatial distribution should be listed;

First of all, students should pay attention to what studied factors have the most influence upon the characteristics of plant communities (they are usually relief and anthropogenic impact). However, analysis of soil and soil-forming rocks' influence should not be ignored, as vegetation is in close connection with the soil and sometimes these factors can serve as the leading ones.

While analyzing the **connection of vegetation with abiotic factors**, students should first analyze the interrelation of plant formations with specific relief elements, mentioning its role in redistribution of warmth and moisture – two ecological factors of the most importance for plant vital functions, as well as their influence upon plant associations within the studies area (mainly on species and ecological composition of communities).

If vegetation is analyzed simultaneously with soil studies, then it is necessary to link all found plant formations with soils, which have formed underneath.

When students characterize **anthropogenic impact**, they should analyze its connection to diversity and patchiness of phytocenoses and influence of human economic activities upon composition of plant formations.

Botanical descriptions of plant formations can be worked out on the basis of date obtained in the course of mapping as additional information.

Description of vegetation in the given area under study can include a different number of topics, which depend on diversity and peculiarities of vegetation cover. On the whole, students can provide an **ecological and coenotic description of detected plant formations** in compliance with the legend where communities belonging to the zonal type of vegetation occupy the first place.

Some general information should be provided prior to a description of plant associations of specific vegetation type.

So the section devoted to **forests** should contain information about what forest types are found in the area (on the map or along the transect line) (i.e. native or derived (secondary), what forest types dominate according to occupied area, what trees they consist of, what forest types are characterized with the most diversity of plant communities.

When describing **meadows**, it is necessary to describe types of meadows, which are plotted on the map or along the transect line: floodplain, continental, among continental meadows students should detect lowland and dry meadows. They should also explain what role meadow communities play in the composition of the vegetation cover in the given areas.

When students start a **description** of a plant association, they should first provide its **full name** and a **number**, which corresponds with the number used for the given plant association in the map legend. They should describe its **location** on the map and provide a **brief description of the habitat**, after that they can write down its ecological description.

The description should be combined and integrated, so students should not list all the parameters from the geobotanical description forms (they are attached to the study report as facts).

When they describe a specific plant association, reference to a corresponding number of the description form should be made. The report should mainly focus on characteristic features of plant formations, i.e. on **striking peculiarities**, which distinguish the community from other vegetative patterns within the given vegetation type.

Thus, when determining ediphicators (species which determine "appearance" of the plant community) and dominants (abundant species), students should underline their **role** in the association. It is not enough to state that crown density is high, students should explain **what** such degree of crown density **results in**, how it influences development and distribution of plants belonging to lower layers, and how it influences the species composition. They should try to **reveal reasons** determining diversity or poor species composition, presence of simple or complex structure. Students should name plant species or specific ecological groups that form certain features of the habitat, such as excess or insufficient moisture, soil reaction, poorness or richness of soils with nutrients, etc.

When analyzing **forest types**, students should pay serious attention to the description of forest renewal, as sustainability and the subsequent community development greatly depends on it. Evaluation of fodder plants should be given for **meadow associations**.

When analyzing **anthropogenic vegetation**, special attention should be paid to the presence and role of weeds, their ecological and biological peculiarities. Students should find out the most abundant species and reveal the connection of weeds with culture as well as the influence of habitat conditions on dockage of fields.

Description of plant associations can be conducted differently depending on how greatly they differ within the limits of a specific vegetation type. Plant associations can be described separately, or several similar associations can be described at the same time: first their common features are noted, and then their distinctive characteristics. There can be no uniform model, as in each case the approach to description of plant associations should be individual.

However, when making a botanical description of studied vegetation cover, it is **necessary**:

1) To mention distribution patterns for all associations found within the studied area;

2) To reveal interrelations of plant formations with physical and geographical factors;

3) To indicate anthropogenic impact;

4) To mark out characteristic ecological and coenotic features of plant associations;

5) To show forming role of specific plant species and plant groups.

In conclusion, students can show economic use of vegetation in the studies area and can briefly touch upon issues of specific plant associations and plant species' protection.

Forest Vegetation Description Form № ______

Date: ______   Authors: ________________________________

Administrative and local position: ____________________________

____

Position in the relief: __________________________________

Surrounding plant associations: __________________________

Described area (м х м): ________________________________

The name of plant association: __________________________

Arboreal and Bush Layers	Crown Density	Formula of the Forest Stand	D (1,3)	H (fs)	H (ca)	Age
Old and Adult Forest Stand						
Young Growth					-	
Understory (Bush Layer)					-	

D (1,3) - diameter of tree trunks measured at chest height (~1.3m) in centimeters, H (fs) – average height of the plants in meters; H (ca) - the height of crown attachment (an average height at which lower living branches of trees are found) (only for the forest stand).

Herbaceous-Shrub Layer

Hillocks: Depressions:

Moss-Lichen Layer

Hillocks: Depressions:

Green plants under snow

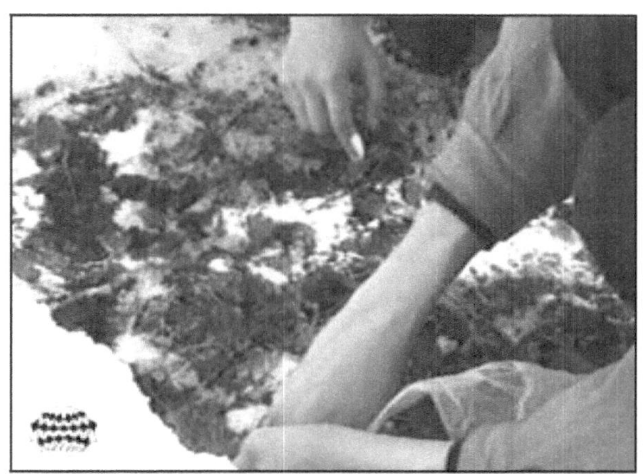

This manual describes how different plants over-winter, different plant adaptations to winter and the difference between evergreen and wintergreen plants. The field study focuses on the study of green plants under the snow cover and includes selection and location of sites, description of vegetation cover and report preparation.

Introduction

This activity is aimed at the study of plants which are found green under snow. It is advised to **choose several biotopes** (habitats) which greatly differ from each other, for instance, *dark-coniferous (spruce) forest, light-coniferous (pine) forest*, deciduous forest and meadow. It is necessary to locate sites in each habitat. All the snow should be dug out from these sites, then all green plants should be counted and determined. The activity will result in lists of species and relative numbers of green plants in different habitats.

Measuring tapes, shovels and plant guidebooks (illustrated ones are preferable) will be required for the lesson.

Prior to practical work, a teacher should start from an introduction into the theme of study, so that students will better understand results of subsequent studies and obtained results. The teacher should discuss with students the problem of life conditions for plants in winter, plant adaptations to unfavorable weather conditions, and classification of plants which winter- green.

Plant adaptations to weather conditions

It is commonly known that winter is a hard and unfavorable season for plants.

Insiccation is the main threat to plants in winter. This is the largest danger, as water in soil gets frozen. If any part of the plant starts drying out in winter, it will inevitably die. As it is known, there is no water transportation within the plant in winter, so it cannot replenish water losses. At the same time, water evaporates well in winter (just remember how quickly fabrics get dry in frost).

Thus all **plant adaptations to winter** are aimed at reduction of water losses. The main method of trees and shrubbery for fighting the dryness of winter is by the abscission of leaves. Plants that employ this method are called deciduous, as all their leaves fall in autumn and live during only one season. The plants receive their necessary amount of light and water in spring and summer, as their large leaves work efficiently enough to provide plants with nutrients for the beginning of the following season. Such plants fall into dormancy in winter as they spend almost no water and do not photosynthesize.

Coniferous plants use another method – there is little water in their needles, as non-freezing essential oils, alkaloids and sugars dominate. All physiological processes in coniferous plants, including photosynthesis, are very slow; however, they can proceed in low temperatures, even in winter. The leaves of coniferous trees evolved into needles, which are quite hard and are protected with a layer of wax in order to minimize water losses. Each leaf (needle) lives for 2-5 years, and they fall not all at the same time, but in turns in the course of a year.

Additional methods of protection for trunks and branches, the *subereous* layer of bark, and bud scales – reduce winter losses of water and ensure long wintering of the mentioned plants.

Delicate herbage is quite another matter. Their main method of survival in winter is by complete dying off of the above-ground part (perennial plants) or the whole plant (annual plants), or special "tangled" adaptations (evergreen and winter-green plants). This lesson will be devoted to the latter two types of plants.

Evergreen and winter-green plants under snow

The main condition of existence of herbaceous green plants in temperate climates is the presence of enough snow cover.

The main function of snow in the given case is protective or heat-insulating. Snow cover has a loose structure due to the shapes of snowflakes. Interstices among snowflakes are filled up with air, which is characterized by low heat conductivity, so we owe such a wonderful property of snow to air. The air, as we sometimes (but incorrectly) say, "is a good insulator."

Due to the low heat conductivity of snow, day-to-day temperature variation penetrates into the snow cover only for a depth of 24 centimeters on average. As specific research has shown, if the amplitude of temperature fluctuation reaches 30 degrees at the snow surface, then at 5 cm depth it amounts to only 16 degrees, whereas at 24 cm depth it makes up 3 degrees and at 44 cm depth the amplitude is insignificant – 0.8 degrees.

Green plants exist in temperate climates in winter due to the presence of snow cover.

How do stunted plants over-winter if they are completely covered with snow?

These plants include dwarf shrubs (they differ from true shrubs only in small size), herbage, mosses and lichens. All of these plants spend winter under far more favorable conditions than trees and bushes. They are found almost completely under protection of the snow cover and they do not tower above it. Winter desiccation and severe frosts pose less threat to those plants. It is not as dangerous to winter under snow cover than it is in open air without any protection.

Most herbaceous plants die off in autumn – either the whole plant (annual plants) or only their above-ground parts (perennial plants). However, there are such plants that are green under snow – their stems and leaves do not change their summer appearance. The stems of those plants are usually not tall, they hardly raise above the ground surface and their leaves are also located near the earth. All above-ground parts of the plants are pressed by the snow cover and are spread flat over the ground surface. Buds also winter on stems beside leaves; young new sprouts will grow out of them next spring. Buds are also located at ground level. In other words, all the above-ground alive parts of the given plants do not rise far above the ground. Frosts and desiccation are not dangerous for the plants as the snow cover protects them securely from winter hardships.

Nevertheless, green grass and bushes also protect themselves from drying out. They have a thin wax coating or pubescence over their leaves as wall as "chemical" protection – special antifreeze properties - tanning agents and sugars from a part of these plant cells. They also have "physical" protection as well – there are some gaps among cells in the tissues of these plants. They help to ensure that freezing water will not tear plant tissue in the manner in which a glass bottle filled with water and is left outside in freezing conditions will.

Two types of plants stay green under snow – **evergreen** (their leaves live for 2-5 years) and **wintergreen** (their leaves live only one year).

Evergreen plants include all *moss species, cowberry, common speedwell, twin-flower and cranberry*. All the plants (except mosses) have a common set of adaptations for all evergreen plants, i.e. small size, cork layer on stems and wax cuticle or pubescence on leaves, high content of non-freezing substances in tissues, etc.

Mosses are a different case. They do not have any problems with wintering as they can winter without snow, completely open. These plants do not have any adaptations to protect them from water losses both in summer and in winter; there is also no protective layer on the surface of their leaves and stems. Mosses do not have to fear severe frosts as drying out is not dangerous for them at all. They do not take up water in the way that many other plants do. Water enters moss not from below, from soil through roots, but mainly from above – out of the atmosphere through leaves and stems.

Mosses do not have true, well-developed roots, so these plants absorb water with their entire above-ground bodies, like a sponge. Moss gives water back the same way, passively, and relatively quickly. Such plants do not have any adaptations for water-keeping. If it has not rained for a long time, moss will lose all the moisture and dry out to an air-dry state. However, it does not die, it merely falls into dormancy. Many other plants, especially larger ones, would certainly die in such a situation. It is an example of surprising adaptation to complete dryness. This unique phenomenon can be explained by specific features of protoplast – the living content of moss cells. The protoplast of mosses does not die even after complete insiccation. Thus, mosses do not fear water losses neither in winter nor in summer. That is why wintering conditions are not of great importance for them. Mosses withstand winters well under any conditions – both under the snow cover and without it.

Wintergreen plants are deciduous plants, which has leaves that appear only in spring (like all of the deciduous plants) and they die off all together, but not in autumn as leaves of all "normal" plants do, but in spring. So leaves live only one year, but the period of their defoliation is in spring.

Advantages of such a life-style are obvious. First, a plant prolongs

its photosynthetic period in that way: from early spring when snow has just melted away until late fall when snow cover becomes thick.

The second reason an interesting one. It is known that all deciduous plants must have a large stock of nutrients for the period when new leaves open. These nutrients are stored by previous "summer" leaves in roots and stems. It takes a long time for normal deciduous plants to develop new sprouts out of stored nutrients. The weather will be sunny and warm for quite some time, but these plants do not immediately start photosynthesizing. It is a shortcoming. Wintergreen plants do not have such a shortcoming. They start photosynthesizing and producing energy as soon as snow melts away, i.e. light comes to them through "old" leaves that have passed the winter. Only after new leaves have appeared will the old leaves die away.

Third, as the leaves of wintergreen plants pass only one winter, they are not like the "armored" as leaves of evergreen plants, which means that they do not cost the plant less (from an energy point of view).

Wintergreen plants which are typical for our forests are **asarabacce**, hairy sedge, prickly-toothed fern, yellow archangel and wood sorrel.

Most evergreen and wintergreen plants are found in spruce forests, if we are speaking about forests of Central Russia. The main reason is the light conditions in lower layers of the forest. A spruce forest is the darkest type of forest, moreover, it is the darkest type in every season. That is why it is so important for plants of the lower layer to prolong photosynthesis as long as possible.

Besides, soils of spruce forests are often not favorable for plants as they are not fertile and usually over-moistened and are characterized with high acidity. Plants develop very slowly under such conditions, leaves come out late in spring, thus old leaves are very important at that time.

There are a great number of wintergreen plants in deciduous forests (but less than in a spruce forest). There is another reason. It becomes so dark under the forest canopy when leaves come out in tree crowns in a deciduous, especially broad-leaved forest, so that many plants cannot develop normally. Many herbaceous plants adapted to very fast development during this short period from snow melt until leaves begin coming out on trees. They adapted in different ways. Some plants – **ephemeroids** – store nutrients in tubers and bulbs and they blossom right after snow melts away (such plants are called primroses and they are studied in Lesson 2, spring), others are wintergreen in order to photosynthesize and produce new sprouts with help from leaves which have passed the winter.

Procedure for collection of material

Fulfillment of the given task is not difficult at all from the methodical

point of view. The task is to select several habitats which greatly differ from each other – in order to reveal interrelations of numbers and species composition of green plants with their growth conditions.

It is advised to study 4-5 habitats – from a dark spruce forest to a meadow association (among them there are *pine forest, mixed forests, small-leafed and broad-leafed forests*).

A site of 1 x 1 m (with the help of a ruler) is chosen in each habitat in a typical place; it is advised to place the site on flat surface. Snow should be removed from the site with the help of a shovel. It is necessary to work with the shovel very carefully while approaching the ground surface so not to damage plants, and the last thin layer of snow should be brushed off with a brush or a broom.

The site cleared from snow is described, i.e. it is necessary to determine species composition of all green plants and their projective cover. If students do not know the names of all green plant species, they should give them conventional names or numbers and collect 2-

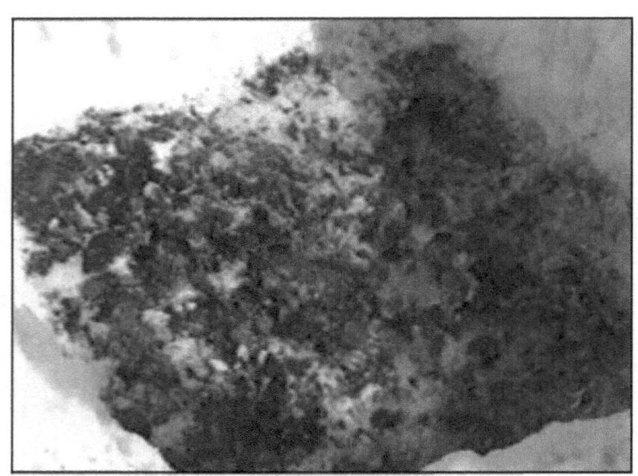

3 specimens of each plant species in order to determine them later in the lab. Plant species should be put separately into different paper bags (envelopes) or bound together with scapes. Then each paper bag (envelope, tuft) should be labeled (when and where it was collected and by whom).

Projective cover is calculated according to a standard procedure. The entire area of the site is taken for 100% and then students determine visually what share of the area is covered with leaves of a separate plant species. Projective cover is estimated as a percentage for each of the found plant species. Unlike in summer, when a meadow community can be multi-layered and the sum of projective covers of all the plants can exceed 100%, it is rather low in winter – from 0.1% to 10 % (and this the case if green plants are found at the site!).

Standard geobotanical description of the habitat is carried out simultaneously with description of the site in its vicinities. Species composition of trees and bushes is determined as usual, their ratio in the forest (formula of the forest stand), crown closure, height and diameter of trees in each forest layer. All data is written down in the description form of the vegetation cover site (see the example at the end of this manual). Procedure for the geobotanical description of a forest and a description form are given in full detail in previous lessons of the given series (Lesson #8, fall, Lesson #4, winter).

Processing and presentation of the results

Processing materials of the given activity is also quite simple and is limited to making a list of different species with their numbers in different studied habitats (in the form of a table). The more habitats have been studied the more interesting the discussion of results will be.

When discussing results of the studies, the following questions should be answered:

1) In which biotope was the maximum number of green plants found (according to a number of species and relative numbers)? Where were there no green plants found?

2) What are the reasons for revealed differences?

3) What types of green plants of those enumerated in the introduction are found and which of them have adaptations to winter?

All collected plants can be presented in the form of a herbarium of evergreen and green plants (the procedure for making a herbarium is given in Lesson #1, summer).

Forest Vegetation Description Form № _______

Date: _______   Authors: _________________________

Administrative and local position: _________________________

____

Position in the relief: _________________________

Surrounding plant associations: _________________________

Described area (м x м): _________________________

The name of plant association: _________________________

____

Arboreal and Bush Layers	Crown Density	Formula of the Forest Stand	D (1,3)	H (fs)	H (ca)	Age
Old and Adult Forest Stand						
Young Growth					-	
Understory (Bush Layer)					-	

D (1,3) - diameter of tree trunks measured at chest height (~1.3m) in centimeters, H (fs) – average height of the plants in meters; H (ca) - the height of crown attachment (an average height at which lower living branches of trees are found) (only for the forest stand).

Herbaceous-Shrub Layer

Hillocks: Depressions:

Moss-Lichen Layer

Hillocks: Depressions:

Methods of Observation of a Chickadee Flock's Territorial Behavior

This manual describes a procedure for observing the territorial behavior of birds of mixed chickadee flocks during autumn and winter. The main of goal is to track the flock's movement within the forest, mapping speed and direction on the flock's route. This data is used for determining the feeding territory of this flock.

Introduction

The study of non-nesting biology of the birds forming mixed chickadee flocks in the forested zone is one of the favorite and most popular topics of individual research of young zoologists.

Mixed chickadee flocks potentially include 10-15 species of small-sized forest birds in Russian forests. They include: 1) *chickadee flocks*, 2) *great tit*, 3) *blue tit*, 4) *crested tit*, 5) *coal tit*. In the north wood zone the *Siberian tit* enters chickadee flocks, in the south and west in broad-leaved forests – the *willow tit*. Besides these basic species, some species, which do not belong to the chickadee family, are, however "full" members of chickadee flocks: 6) *goldcrest*, 7) *bottle tit (long-tailed tit)* 8) *pika*, and 9) *nuthatch*. Moreover, some "accompanying" species are also met in chickadee flocks: 10) *great spotted woodpecker* 11) *lesser-spotted woodpecker (barred woodpecker)* and, sometimes the *three-toed woodpecker.* Woodpeckers, as a rule, enter chickadee flocks for short periods of time – while the flock, migrating along the forest, passes through woodpecker's habitat.

Study of a chickadee flock's biology can be a very rewarding subject for the individual studies of schoolchildren. First, this study does not require great knowledge of all wintering bird species (as for example, a bird census) – only two or up to six species are to be determined, which are distinctive at long-term observations. Second, the procedure of observations is simple and does not require great attention or practical skills. Third, observations of chickadee flocks train student attention, teaching how to visually identify birds in nature. Fourth, while observing, pupils have a chance "to get closely introduced" to studied species, as long-term observed birds get used to people and begin to let them come nearer (up to 1 meter). Fifth, when studying the route of the flock's migrations in the forest, pupils learn to work with a map, define distances on location and determine directional orientation. Last, observations of chickadee flocks use inherent "hunting excitement."

All of the above allow teachers to use an elementary procedure of mapping a chickadee flock's territorial movement in the forest with children in nature. The goal of this study is to mark the habitat (territory) of a chickadee flock on the map and study the peculiarities of the flock's (as a formed group) behavior.

General Information

Period of observations

Observations of the biology of birds that form mixed chickadee flocks are possible during a large part of year - from July until March or April.

Only a short nesting period is excluded from the potential observation time. At this time, flocks get separated because birds form pairs. But when young birds first fly out at the end of the reproductive period, observations become possible again.

The **best time** for organizing an observation of a flock's territorial behavior is late autumn and winter (November - February). At this time, birds form groups that are consistent in structure and, which is very important, in constant territories. The size of these territories depends on forest type, and varies from 5 up to 50 hectares in central Russia. Therefore, observation of the flocks are not as laborious as in summer or early autumn, when birds migrate for long distances and the process of observation can turn out to be quite physically difficult as birds move in the forest with different speeds (either slowing down or accelerating). Besides, in early autumn not all flocks have their "constant" sites, (as, for example, in winter) and some attempts to trace a flock in the forest can be unsuccessful.

There is one more advantage of the fall/winter period; it is rather warm weather, therefore children can work with a map and record data without getting too cold (which is a greater problem in winter). Lack of deep snow cover also makes moving in the forest easier.

Selection of observation site

Because this educational task sets up an objective of mapping a chickadee flock's migration routes in the forest (its "tracking"), it is **necessary to have a map** of this area for the site where the observations are to be conducted. It is better to have a map of the area not less than 1 square kilometer. The preferable map scale is 1:5000 (in 1 cm - 50 meters) or larger.

The observation starts by traveling to the forest site where chickadee flocks are met more often (some preliminary "exploring" excursions are required), if a map of those sites is available. The best places for observation are sites in mixed forests with numerous well visible landmarks - glades, electric-power transmission lines, openings in the forest. Such observations can also be conducted on the forest sites that adjoin vast open spaces - fields, large reservoirs etc. An ideal variant is to conduct tracking on a standard census site or within a forest block (for example, 500m x 500m). In early autumn, however, when the flocks migrate for long distances, it is not necessary, because they will surely fly out of the site limits.

Selection of an object for observation

It is **preferable to observe one-species flocks**, they are "more quiet," migrate slower; break up into smaller groups less often. In the central part of Russia it can be flocks of an average strip (band); it can be marsh tits' or crests' flocks, or their mixed flocks. The numbers of birds in these flocks vary from 5 up to 20, depending on biotope and time of year (in the mixed forest and in early autumn flocks are bigger, whereas in one-species forests and closer to winter they are smaller). Often marsh tits' and crests' flocks also include other species: great tit, blue tit, crested tit, coal tit, long-tailed tit and accompanying species: pika, and nuthatch structure.

A good object for observations on the given subject is long-tailed tits' flocks. However, these birds are mostly found in forests with broad-leaved tree species or near a water body. In addition, their flocks are quite active, migrate for great distances and observations of them turn out to be at a continuous run. On the other hand, long-tailed tits are easily visible (since they feed, basically, on deciduous trees) and have loud enough and, importantly, very characteristic voices - they are well seen and heard from far away.

It is undesirable to select as an object of supervision large mixed flocks consisting of different species from the list and with more than 20 specimens. Such flocks are, as a rule, not stable. They are "noisy" and move in the forest unevenly (by "jerks"), they often break up and aggregate again. It is extremely difficult, even for an experienced ornithologist, to follow these flocks. As a whole, it is easier to work with flocks of smaller size.

Technique for Observation of Flock's Territorial Behavior

Observations can start as soon as a flock is observed. It is better to conduct observations with **three people**.

One has to constantly observe birds' migrations within tree crowns, trying to move in the forest together with a main group of birds. The **second** member of the team has to count the distance covered by a flock by counting steps or with the help of a pedometer.

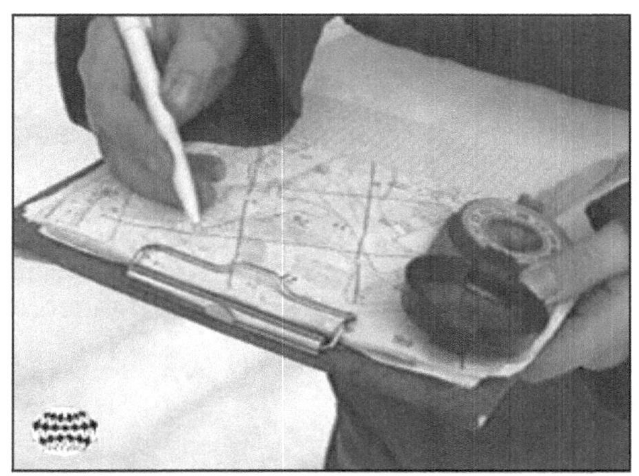

The **third** participant should note the time, map the flock's migration route (and observation team), get oriented by the map and ask the second participant covered distance each time when a sharp turn is made or every five minutes when moving in a straight line. If the responsibilities in the group are distributed precisely and each participant executes only his or her duties, and if tracking the flock passes smoothly, the duration of observation can constitute 2-3 hours, and the total length of the mapped route, 2-3 km.

Before observations, each participant should measure the length of their steps, so that it is possible to define distances on location. It is also necessary to have some knowledge of the birds that can form chickadee flocks in the observation area in order to be able to define species composition and number of birds in the watched flock. The third participant working with a map should have a watch.

The **allocation of responsibilities within the research group** should be kept consistent, at least through one day. In fact, competency in each skill (flock observation, measuring distance, or mapping the route) is not formed quickly, but after some time (approximately in one hour of "net observation"). Some first attempts, as a rule, fail - observers lose the flock out of sight, or "lose" their

position on a map, or are mistaken in measuring distances. Only after several attempts, the observers at last begin to execute their functions more easily.

Out of the three participants, the most complicated duties are the duties of an "observer." This participant should have good vision and should be able to be very active. He or she should monitor the "core" of the flock, i.e. a group of the most active and "noisy" birds, which lead all other birds by all possible means. The observer should try to constantly watch the core's movement in crowns, trying to "predict" the general direction of its migration. Bird flocks found in the forest usually move with a low speed (1-2 km per hour) i.e., the speed of very slow pace. From time to time, however, birds sharply accelerate their speed (at a transition from one biotope to another, or when meeting another flock), so that it is necessary to run after them in order to catch up with the flock. The observer should catch up with the flock constantly by all means, without paying any attention to or communicating with other participants of the group. The other participants, during such "intense" moments, should not pay attention to birds but in fact, map the observer's running route.

During "quiet" periods en route, the second and third participants of the group should not go "tailgating" after the observer; they should keep some distance (20-30 m) behind.

Presentation of results

The scheme of the flock's route in the forest should be the end result (fig. 1), or a large-scaled map with a drawn route - with marks of times when the flock passed landmarks (glades, roads, borders of the forest etc.) and with 5-minute marks along the route. In addition, route sections that were covered by a flock at different speeds can be marked with lines of various thicknesses. Route sections where the flock moved slowly can be marked with thick lines, whereas sections covered at high speed - by a thin line. Transitions should be made with smooth lines.

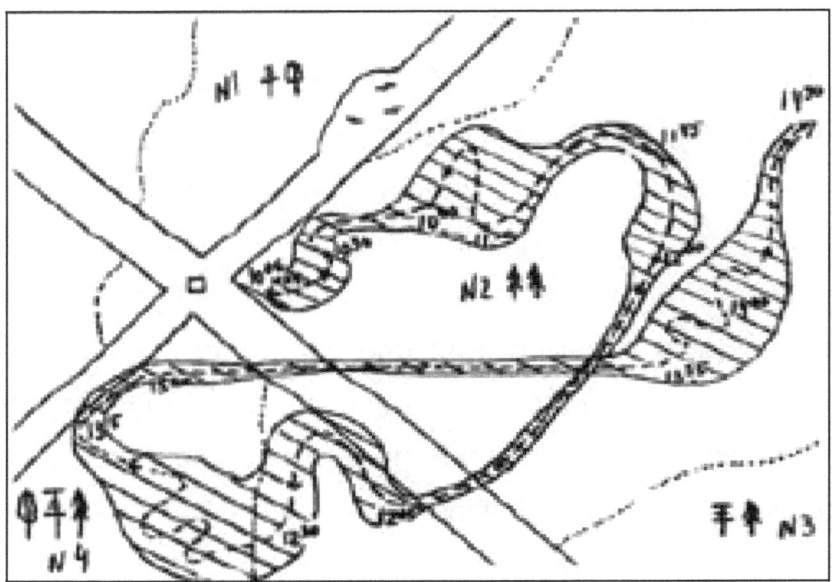

Fig. 1. Example of observation results presentation

In analyzing the results, it is necessary to attempt to explain found regularities - whether the flock returns to the same place, what the total territory used by the flock is, why the speed of the flock's movement in different forest sites vary, how birds behave at transitions from one biotope to another or upon meeting other flocks.

If sufficient "labor resources" are available (more than one group of trained observers) and if there are more than one distinctive forest type (for example, coniferous and deciduous forests) it is possible to conduct flock observations in each habitat separately, or to conduct observations of flocks consisting of different bird species and then compare the results (flocks' composition, form and area of the territory, speed and character of movements in the forest, etc).

Procedure of winter mammals route census by footprints

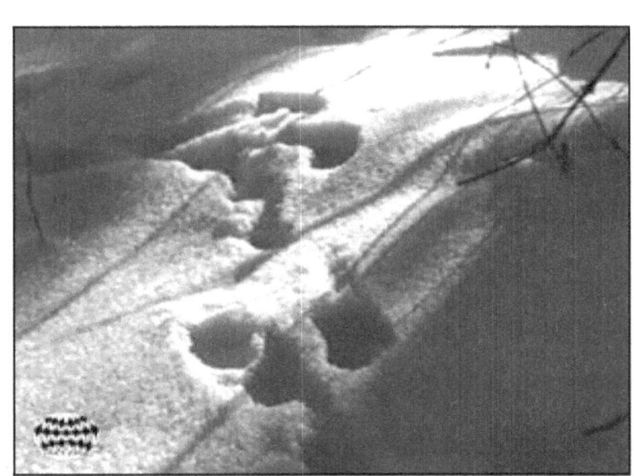

This manual contains a standard procedure of census for large and middle-sized mammals (from weasel to elk) during a winter period, which is applied in the system game animals' census in the forested zone of Russia. This manual includes a description of census routes selection procedure, technique of census data processing and calculation of numbers of animals per unit of the area.

Introduction

The educational task described here leads to students individual route census of animals using footprints left by mammals on snow cover during winter. According to the task, several censuses are made separately in three or four types of habitats most typical for your area.

This work is not too laborious, however, it requires the skill to recognize animal species by their footprints, skills to get orientated and to measure distances on location, as well as skiing ability.

Main idea of procedure of winter mammals route census by footprints

In Russia the winter route census is applied to an estimation of *population density* and numbers of average and large mammals on large territories. It is also used with scientific research purposes within the *venatic* (venatorial, hunting) system.

The **procedure** of winter route census is based on estimations that the average number of mammal footprints crossing a registration route is directly proportional to this species' population density. Whereas a number of footprints within the area depends on activity of animal migrations (movements): the probability of finding animal footprints en route is higher the more active the animal is and the more it migrates.

Thus, in order to **estimate** the species' population density (number of specimens per unit of the area) two parameters are required: 1) an average of footprint crossings made by an animal per a time unit (for example, per one day) per unit of route length and 2) a coefficient connected with mobile activity (length of a daily course) of the given animal.

In a simple example, the formula of population density estimation based on the data from counting footprints as $D = A\,K$, where D equals the given species' population density (number of animals per unit of the area within the territory), A equals census value (average of footprint crossings made by animals of a certain species during one day per a unit of route length), and K equals conversion factor, connected with length of a daily course of the animal during the census period in the given territory.

In this connection, the census procedure consists of two parts: 1) determination of "A" value, i.e. direct route counting 2) estimation of conversion factor K.

The conversion factor can be determined by one of the following methods: 1) by tracking animals' footprints with the subsequent estimation of an average length of a daily course, 2) by comparison of a census value with an animals' population density on the test sites; thus the number of animals on test sites is defined by the method of multiday encirclement.

In order to **calculate the conversion factor** correctly, it is necessary to use the information on an average length of a daily course of animals received by various methods in different years in different regions. It is very time-consuming work; therefore, nowadays the calculation of conversion factors is carried out only by state statistic organizations. In Table 2 (see at the end of this manual) the average values of factors for the majority of animal species inhabiting forested zones of Russia calculated for three main climatic zones based on the research data in 1991-1994 are indicated.

These factors can be used for the purposes of the given educational task only in the case that similar factors of animals' daily activity for your area are not available.

Census procedure

Conditions of census

The main condition of a winter route census is the presence of snow cover, on which animals leave their footprints.

Census taking is not carried out during a period of hard frosts, long thaws, in a period when ice crust is formed on the snow surface, or during days with a strong wind, snowfall or drifting snow. Thus, a census does not take place during days with **"extreme" weather conditions**. After a heavy snowfall the census is not carried out for 2-3 days.

If a strong snowfall or blizzard starts after footprints have been cleaned from the route or while a census is being taken, the census stops and should be carried out again when good weather returns. Do not bring a dog to the census taking; in addition, do not use a car or move along frequently used roads.

Census technique

The census is carried out during two days.

On the first day *(day to clean footprints)* counters walking along the route clean all the crossing footprints, so that when going along the route again the next day, only newly appeared, fresh footprints are counted.

Cleaning footprints is done the following way: a wide spruce or pine branch is attached (knotted) to the belt of a counter, who skies along the route. The branch moves behind the counter and cleans all old footprints. As the result a "footprints registering strip"1-2 meters wide is formed behind the counter.

Animal **tracks** should be **covered** with snow so that the next day, the number of animals that have passed through can be counted. If when cleaning footprints you find footprints of large rare predators (wolf, lynx, etc.), the number of each species' footprints that cross the route should be counted and recorded in the notebook

On the second day *(day to count footprints),* going strictly along the same route, the counters record either in their notebooks or on the map of the route, all new footprints crossing the route, specifying

the species and number of animals that left the footprints. If an animal (wolf, fox etc.) came to a ski-track, and then carefully turned back, it is recorded as one crossing of the route. When animal footprints are found that came along the same tack (a trace in a trace), it is necessary to pass along track to the place where the animals divided and then calculate their exact number. When numerous footprints are met on along a short route section (for example, at feeding) the total number of footprint crossings at the section is recorded.

The length of the route is measured on a map or directly when going along the route (by counting steps).

Habitat isolation

In the hunting system when conducting winter route census, all habitats are subdivided into three categories - "forest," "swamp," and "field."

"Forest" corresponds to woods of different ages, including those in swamps. It also corresponds to forest clearings, glades, deforestation sites, burned-out places, and shrub thickets.

"Swamp" corresponds only to open swamps or those with suppressed growth of trees (shorter than a person's height). Open swamps can be found among woods or among fields – they also refer to "swamp."

"Field" includes all other open areas: plowed lands, pastures, hayfields, meadows, and tundra.

When conducting this educational task, such **subdivision of the territory** can lay down a foundation, however, if it is possible (meaning, some groups of counters are available), habitat isolation can be quite different. For example, more categories can be defined with the definition of several forest types, depending on their age and species composition.

Measurement of the route length

Length of the census route can be measured on a large-scale map, forestry plan, plan of land management, or map of the hunting territory. The route is laid down on a map and its length is measured with a ruler, ***curvometer (hodometer)*** or a divider.

If the route is laid on a forest quarter network plan, the length can be measured along quarters, knowing the distance between cutting glades. The length of the route can be first measured in the number of steps with further calculations in meters.

Routes location and census volume

The census routes in the studied region are chosen based on an approximate proportional **scope of the habitats available** on the given territory. The simplest method to achieve such proportionality is to lay an even network of routes on the territory of the region, paying attention that sites relatively poor in animals are not excluded from the census.

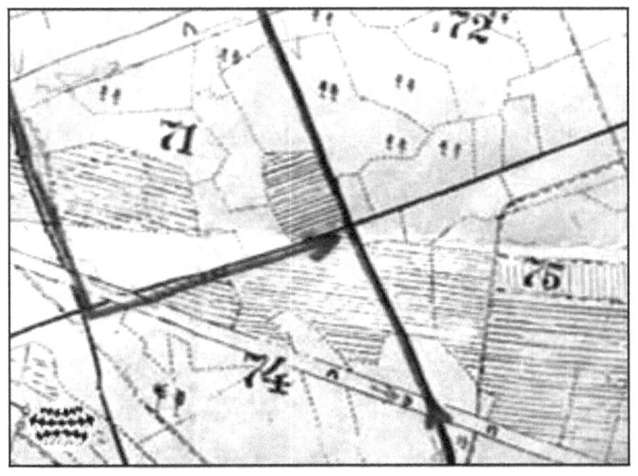

The route can be both unidirectional and closed, depending on the convenience of the passage. Each route should consist of a number of straight-line sections or be entirely rectilinear. The routes should not bypass open areas (including central parts of large fields and swamps), and should cross them according to the basic direction. The routes should not pass along roads, wide glades, along the rivers and streams, forest margins, ridges, creek valleys or gullies.

For the purposes of the given educational task it is necessary to study not less than three to four of the most typical habitats in your area. The census should cover not less than 5 kilometers in each of them.

Processing results

Calculation of numbers

After all seasonal works are complete; all census **results are consolidated** in one final table (Table 1), where data on the total number of each species' footprint crossings are registered for each habitat during all days of the census.

Table 1. Example of the final table cap for the calculation of animals' population density based on the results of winter census of footprints in three biotopes (1- forest, 2 - swamp and 3 - field)

	Animals species	Total length of routes (km)			Total number of footprint crossings			Number of crossings per 1 route km (census value)			Animal population density (specimens per 1 sq. km)		
		1	2	3	1	2	3	1	2	3	1t	2	3
1													
2													
3													
...													

Then the **total number of footprints** crossings per 1 km of a route is calculated (a census value). In order to do this, the total number of footprint crossings in the given habitat is divided by a corresponding total route length passed in this habitat (in kilometers).

For further data processing the received census value is multiplied by a conversion factor (from Table 2) and the received value of population density in specimens per 1 square kilometer is written in the appropriate column of the table. This value is the final (end) result of the conducted winter route census. For the greater presentation it is possible to calculate the final value of density not per 1, but per 10 square kilometers, since the numbers of some animals when calculated per 1 sq. Km will appear fractional.

On the back of the final table or in the separate appendix, a copy of the regional map of the region with marked census routes and scheme of main habitats distribution should be submitted.

Table 2. Conversion **factors for the winter route census of animals** (Average data on 49 administrative regions of the Russian Federation from 1991-1994).

Animal species	Northern regions (deep snow zone)	Central regions (moderate snow zone)	South regions (less snow zone)
Squirrel	4.5	5.2	5.2
Wolf	0.11	0.1	0.09
Weasel	1.3	1.6	1.7
Mountain hare	1.2	1.2	1.2
European hare	0.6	0.6	0.5
Boar	0.6	0.55	0.5
Siberian weasel	0.9	0.9	0.9
Corsac	0.24	0.24	0.24
Roe deer	0.69	0.64	0.64
Marten	0.6	0.70	0.95
Fox	0.23	0.21	0.18
Elk (Moose)	0.85	0.75	0.65
Red deer	0.68	0.68	0.68
Axis deer	0.72	0.72	0.72
Glutton	0.11	0.11	0.11
Lynx	0.22	0.22	0.22
Sable	0.43	0.43	0.43
Polecat (Fitch)	0.8	0.7	0.6

Note: Conversion factors, indicated in the table, cannot be applied unconditionally in the scientific purposes to all regions of a wood zone and in various winter weather conditions. They are approximate and can be used only with educational/research purposes when working with the schoolchildren.

Study of Mammal Ecology According to Their Tracks

This manual provides a procedure for "tracking" mammals according to tracks left in the snow. Focus is on the behavior of mammals: size of their habitat, biotopic and habitat distribution, feeding sites, behavior during feeding, etc. Several methods of determining track freshness, the direction of movement and rules for tracking are described.

Introduction

Snow cover, which replaces autumn's leaves and mud, provides zoologists with an opportunity to delve into **undercover details of animal life**, especially mammals, including the most careful and reserved ones. Any beast, regardless of its size, leaves tracks on the snow surface, in other words "an autograph" on loose snow, especially newly fallen snow.

An observer who has certain **pathfinder's skills** (which can and should be mastered over time,) learns what animals the tracks belong to and under what conditions they have been left. If one follows the whole route (track route) of an animal, recording carefully all evidence impressed on snow, then it is possible to precisely describe all features of animal life in quantitative indicators at the given section of the route.

The given lesson involves independent students' work in "tracking" animals that inhabit the vicinities of the school or a field study center, which leave tracks on the snow. They are mainly mammals characterized as active in winter. They include *hoofed animals: elk, deer, wild boars, roe deer; Lagmorpha: brown hare and Alpine hare; rodents: squirrels, muskrats, beavers, Carnivore: wolves, foxes, raccoons, lynx; martens, minks, polecats, ermine, weasels, otters and wolverines.*

The task involves tracking several (different) individuals belonging to one or several animal species out of the mammals found in the given area.

A **map of the area** where tracking will take place is required (a large-scale map is preferable), as well as rulers, compasses and field notebooks.

Essentials of the tracking procedure

The **tracking procedure** generally consists of the following: an observer goes along a chain of animal footprints "to the toes" (in the same direction as the animal) or "to the heel" (against the animal movement); the observer is not allowed to cut off any loops or turnings made by an animal, as hunters usually do. The distance covered is counted in steps, whereas the direction of each turn is measured according to the compass. All the data is recorded in the field notebook or plotted on the available plan of the site. At the same time, students should register all of the important features of the animal's behavior.

What are tracks? Determination and measurement of tracks

Preliminary excursions, study of literature, photos and drawings of animal tracks and practical training aimed at familiarization with tracks of major animal species in the given area will help students to master practical skills of track determination. Data on relative numbers of different animal species and skills in track determination that have been gained in the previous lesson will make selecting the object of study much easier.

The given educational task involves dealing not only with tracks in their classical representation, i.e. footprints of paws, but with other traces of vital animal functions left on snow as well.

Traces of vital functions are usually considered as follows:

1. *Trails of movement* – footprints of paws or other parts of a body (a tail, a belly), broken shrubs, compacted paths, littering caused by animal's movement through branches and thickets.

2. *Traces of feeding activity* – food debris and food reserves, digging in snow, traces of a search for food, feeding tables, bitten and broken plants, traces of chasing and dragging of prey, etc.

3. *Tracks associated with shelter-making* – burrows, lairs, lies, passages under the snow, etc.

4. *Traces of life functions* – excrement, urinary spills, traces of molting and hair shedding.

5. *Information tracks* – traces of information-passing which indicate occupancy of the area – bite marks and scratches on trees and on the ground, discharge of musky glands, sound signals.

It is necessary to remember that tracks of a group of animals are

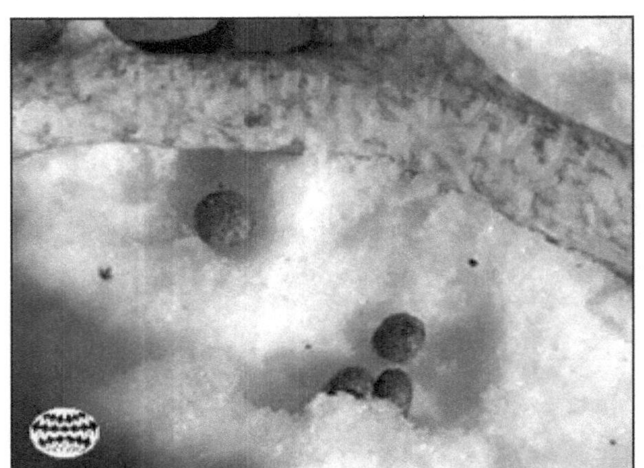

almost never found just as they are, for instance, trails of movement can be associated with search for food, whereas urinary spills usually mark the area.

Familiarization with tracks allows the determination of the species of animal that has left them. Large-size animals can be easily recognized according to specific separate footprints of paws or hoofs. Footprints of small-size animals are quite another matter. They are usually so unclear and similar to traces of other species that it is more reliable to be guided by the evaluation not of separate footprints but by chains of tracks. One should take into account characteristic features of movements, procuring food, habits and other behavioral peculiarities.

The following **external features of traces** are significant for the determination of an animal species: contours of footprints, presence of prints of claws and *calcaneal* calluses, distance of footprints from one to another in the direction of motion.

Students often have to take different kinds of **measurements** when tracking animals. It is more convenient with the help of a short ruler or a folding rule. Soft "tailor's" measuring tapes are less appropriate. When measuring footprints, the ruler should be held balanced exactly above the trace or put on the snow next to it, but not on the footprint itself, as it can damage the footprint. When finding a single footprint, it is recommended to measure its maximum width and length, including the nail prints.

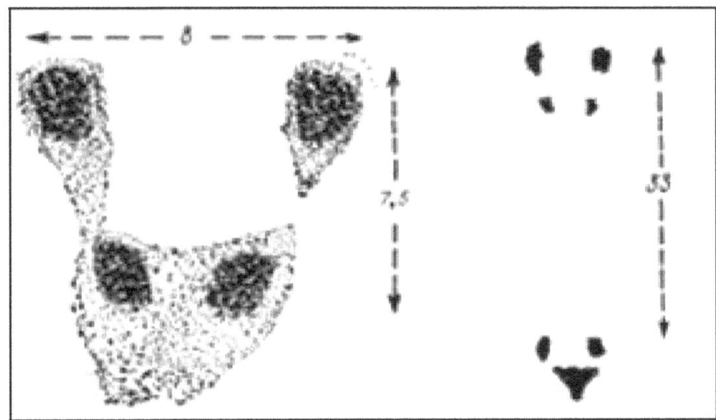

The length of a jump is determined between two like footprints, i.e. either between two left ones or between two right ones, starting from the front edge of the footstep as it is usually clearer than the back one. Sometimes (in the case of rodents) it is necessary to measure the distance among all four footprints in their group.

Besides the animal species, it is important to determine freshness of tracks and direction of the animal's motion. It is preferable to deal with fresh traces, which have just been left or were left the night before. Sometimes, however, old traces can also be used, especially when studying tracks of large-sized animals. Many characteristics should be taken into account in order to define the age of tracks.

How to determine freshness of a footprint

Two main factors are taken into account when determining the freshness of tracks: **behavioral biology of the animal** (its diurnal activity) and **weather conditions**. For instance, if the animal is active at night and snowfall finished last evening, but footprints are not covered with a layer of snow, then they are less than one day old.

It is advised to conduct mammal tracking on fresh-fallen snow.

There are different types of fresh-fallen snow. If snowfall finished in the evening, it is called **"long" fresh-fallen snow**: animals managed to leave traces of their night activity. Such weather is the most interesting for a pathfinder-researcher.

"Short" newly-fallen snow means snowfall consequences which ended at the second half of the night. In this case, there are footprints of animals that return to their lairs from chasing after prey or from feeding. This snow is a favorite type of snow for hunters; however, it is not the best for a researcher.

If it has been snowing for the whole night and it stopped snowing only in the morning – it is called **"dead" newly-fallen snow** –as there are almost no tracks left under such weather conditions.

It is quite difficult to conduct the tracking of mammals when there are **too many traces** – i.e. it means that there has been no snowfall for several days and there are a great number of traces left on the snow of different prescriptions and of different kinds.

For valid tracking it is advised to follow a newly (not more than one day old) track after "long" newly-fallen snow, as it is possible to follow the whole diurnal (night) course of animal's movement: from lair to lair, even though this can take much time.

The following rules also apply for the determination of trace **freshness**:

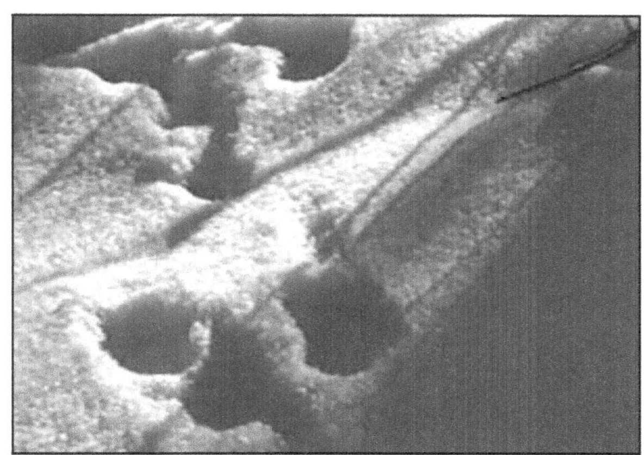

1). Fresh traces look crisp on deep snow cover in sunny weather. If even the smallest details of tracks are well seen including prints made by claws or the edges of hoofs and thrown snow is delicate and looks like foam, it means that an animal has just been there!

2) Try traces by touch. Fresh tracks in dry snow are soft like fluff in hard frost. Edges of the footprint get gradually covered with a thin crust of ice in the course of time; the older the trace is, the harder it is. Tracks harden slightly in 15-20 minutes when it is 10 degrees of frost. If it is 15-20 degrees of frost, traces harden in five minutes. A thin crust of ice appears very quickly over deep footprints of large-sized mammals (elk). Tracks of light animals with surface footprints (mice, ermine) do not harden at all – it is impossible to determine their freshness by touch. Tracks of hares harden rather well.

3). Try to intersect tracks with the help of a thin twig: it will cut fresh tracks (10-15 min) almost without bending; it will cut but will bend at old tracks (5-10 hours), however, it will not cut very old traces (a day old and older) as it will slip out of them.

4) It is possible to lift up a footprint by pushing a hand under it. Fresh tracks will fall into pieces; older ones will remain like a snowball in the hand. The thickness of the snowball will be greater the older the tracks are.

5) When it is 15-20 degrees of frost, animal urine keeps its natural color in the snow for 1.5-2 hours, and then it darkens. The snow that has been wet with urine falls into small pieces in an hour and then it is frozen back together in 3-4 hours. Droppings remain soft even when it gets covered with hoarfrost. The surface of droppings is frozen in 1-2 hours and frozen solid in 3 hours.

6) It is possible to leave your own marks and traces in snow in protected places in order to control rate of track changes. Then it is necessary to watch their changes over time and compare the changes with found tracks.

How to determine the direction of an animal's movement

If snow cover is not deep or if it is wet, tracks are printed clearly and it is not difficult to determine the direction of an animal's movement. When prints of claws, finger-pads or hooves are not seen in loose and deep snow, you can apply the following techniques:

1) Compare length of **dragging out** (the front edge of the footprint, i.e. in the direction of movement) and dragging behind (the back edge). The latter is always longer than the dragging out, as the foot is

always put into snow gently sloping, whereas it is dragged out much more steeply;

2) **Snow burst** can be seen at the front edge of the footprint – a roller is a little higher than the general level of the snow cover, especially if tracks are fresh;

3) **Touch** edges of several tracks – the front edge is always harder than back ones, as when an animal pulls out a paw, it presses it, so the snow is fused into a frozen mass when aging;

4) **Watch** the general appearance of the tracking path; try to imagine an animal's movements. When you see changes in step length in front of an obstacle, traces of climbing onto or jumping off, you will understand logic of the animal's motion and, correspondingly, its direction.

Main paces of animals

When tracking, students often have to record the different paces (gaits) of animals. Here are some of them:

1) *Slow pace* – a footprint of the back paw is placed behind and on one side of the front paw's print;

2) *Round pace* – a footprint of the back paw falls exactly into the footprint of the front paw;

3) *Trot* – a footprint of the back paw can be in front of the front paw's print. These traces are characteristic of hoofed animals and Carnivores of the dog and cat families;

4) ***Two-step, three-step and four-step*** – it is a gallop when tracking groups consist of two, three or four footprints. It is a typical gait of the marten family and it depends on the running speed.

5) ***Full gallop*** – footprints of back paws are far in front of the front ones – it is a characteristic way of hare and squirrel movement. Other animals usually use full gallop at forced cases of speeding-up (flight, chase).

Tracking procedure

First a group of observers, which usually consists of two people, simply looks for appropriate tracks of a desired animal species.

When they find traces, they start moving against the animal's movement. Of course, it is tempting to follow an animal, trying to catch up with it and watch it. However, we are not talking about hunting, when all thoughts are aimed at running down and killing an animal. Research purposes are quite different. It is usually worthwhile to give up the idea of watching an animal, for we might frighten it off, so it is preferable to go against the animal's movement. It allows students to study behavior of a calm animal and to follow its movement to the very beginning – along (night or) day lies.

Later, when this section of the route is over, it is possible to come back to the starting point and continue tracking, this time in the same direction as an animal has gone. When there are several groups of students it is possible to conduct animal tracking simultaneously in both directions.

Thus, as a result, students will come up with a clear notion of the whole distance covered by an animal and they end up with many interesting observations, which will be most valuable if they are properly recorded and qualitatively processed later.

Study of animal behavior in the course of tracking

Features of winter distribution of a certain animal species are revealed as the result of tracking according to its habitats, character of shelters, ways of moving depending upon circumstances and specificity of distribution and structure of the snow cover. Balance of feeding and many other aspects of animal behavior can also be evaluated.

Studying **hares and hoofed animals**, the following information should also be taken down: what trees and shrubs they usually gnaw around and nibble; each time it is observed it is necessary count the number of bite marks. Then the degree of damage should be determined; in particular, all broken specimens are recorded, eaten plants found under snow cover should be registered as well as the size of digging marks made by the animal. All sites of urination and excretion are recorded; sometimes the number of feces ("scat") should be counted in order to determine the degree of eaten feed assimilation.

Special attention is paid to conditions of movement depending on depth, density and features of distribution of the snow cover. Finally, all sites and peculiarities of lies are recorded.

It goes without saying that all interesting findings and observations made according to tracks are written down in the **tracking report**. Records are kept with different degrees of specification depending on working conditions (in particular, on frost, freshness, depth and density of snow cover), on distance covered by an animal as well as on abundance of facts in the course of tracking

As experience shows, it is more convenient to conduct tracking in **teams of two**: one (leading) observer determines the direction of the animal's movement and all its turns according to the compass; this observer registers all crossed habitats and counts steps from one lie to another. It is important to measure the depth of the animal's footprints and depth of the snow cover regularly with help of a ski pole, which is marked from the top end with sections five and ten cm long. Determination of snow cover density, its structure, presence of thin crust of ice over snow and buried ice crusts are also of great importance. The second observer watches closely for bitten trees and bushes and counts the bite marks.

The lengths of different sections of an animal's path are recorded in the tracking protocol – in steps or in meters. Sites where an animal fed should be marked with a letter "f" (feeding), unlike free movement.

Records in the field notebook may look as follows:

Forest Clearing

NW, 35 f, droppings, (85), 50 f, lie, droppings (105).

NE, 20 f, 50, droppings, (95), 35 f, lie, urinat.

Mixed forest

NE, 30f, droppings, (95).

Records are kept brief; words are replaced with separate letters or even conventional signs. It is useful to register different details of an animal's behavior that have not been recorded in the main protocol.

The second observer, as we have already mentioned, registers bite marks and fodders. In the simplest case, this observer can be limited to counting only the number of bushes and trees that are gnawed around. However, such data is too sketchy; it does not take into account the degree of damage or the amount of plants eaten. Feeding can be more accurately characterized if all gnawed sprouts on each damaged tree are counted, and if bitten bark and broken tops of trees are registered. Such work is, of course, time-consuming, but it ensures excellent results.

However, it is necessary to bear in mind that only newly made fodders and bite marks should be counted. If tracking is carried out in clear sunny weather and in frost, they are easily noted by their white color and lack of hoarfrost at the sharp bend. When the weather is warmer and overcast, it is rather difficult to determine the standing of the damage, especially if there is a lack of time or experience.

Counting fodders and covered distance is conducted from a lie to another lie. The exact number of sprouts and bark, which have been eaten up at the given section becomes known due to the mentioned fact, so that number in comparison with the number of droppings allow the observers to determine the food balance of the animal.

Tracking **predatory animals**, in particular, the small species that are usually found, is characterized with certain peculiarities. It is especially important to register its ways of procuring food: coming under wind-fallen trees, under roots and low tree branches, dives into snow, catching prey and unsuccessful attempts at chasing prey; quick jumps and turns, changes in pace, use of forest roads, ski-tracks, animal paths, climbing on trees and jumps from one tree crown to another one; "mining" of the snow cover, sites of lies, excretion and urination.

Some researchers advise to count and record traces of predatory animals' activity after each hundred steps covered, whereas when tracking of larger beasts of prey – record each 500 or even 1000-1500 steps. It seems, though, that it is more reliable to register events immediately so not to forget details and it is even better to map the covered distance at the same time.

When plotting the animal's route on a map it is recommended to use conventions for different forms of the animal's activity, for instance: ᴑ - urination, • - droppings, ■ - lie, ⊗ - catching prey, Ø - unsuccessful chase, ♦ -feeding, etc.

A **system of conventions** can also be used for the animal's different ways of movement, for instance: → - single-line tracks, ⇒ - double tracks, ↔ - single-line tracks in both directions, ⇔ - double tracks in both directions, ≡ - path, ≠- intersection of the path with tracks, and so on.

Similar techniques for observation of behavior with the help of the tracking method are successfully applied not only of predators of the marten family, but also when studying the ecology of **small forest rodents**. Study of these animals' tracks usually involves limited sites, as Muridae (simple-toothed rodents) make only short rushes from one tree or bush to another. A detailed mapping of corresponding sites on a large scale can depict such characteristic habits better. It is advised to conduct mapping in strips of one meter wide, which are consecutively marked out in the site devoted for survey. Ski poles, marked in decimeters, can be used there. It is easier to draw borders of sites and separate strips for mapping on the snow surface with the help of ski poles.

One interesting technique of direct observation of rodents in under-snow passages is by digging trenches of 20-25 meters long and half a meter wide, which are deep to the ground (to the ground cover). Such a trench crosses under-snow rodents' passages. Wooden slats are fixed on trench walls at the height of the damaged tunnel to restore the rodents' passage. Slats resemble cross-planked footways. Rodents use them freely and they appear in observer's field of vision when crossing the trench. The observer should stand at one of the trench ends.

Processing the tracking results

Tracking itself is just a procedure for studying an animal species, its

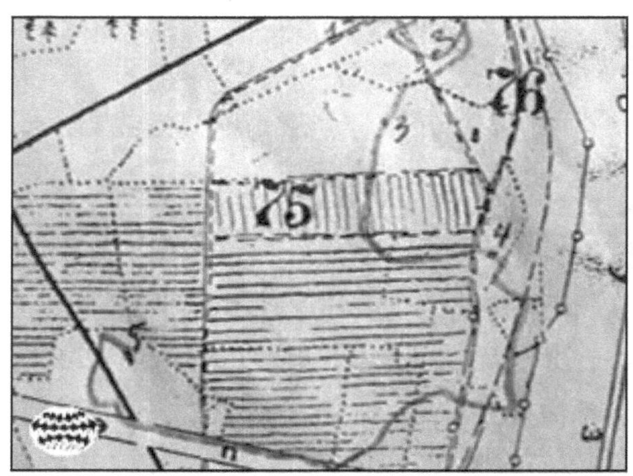

behavior and ecology. The results of tracking require quantitative processing.

The first is to determine the **quantitative index** that comes from tracking results is size of animal's habitat or length of the animal's diurnal (night) movement. This index is calculated on the basis of made map or records in the field notebook. If students conducted observations of animal, which lives settled (elks, boars, squirrels), then it is advised to plot the tracking route on the map and to determine area of the site according to the map. If the animal inhabits very large territory and it moved more or less straight along the whole section of tracking, then students can limit their calculation to the distance covered by the animal.

The second index is **calculation of different forms of animal behavior per unit** of its route. It is necessary to count all the typical forms of animal activity – feeding sites and chasing area (separately for successful an unsuccessful ones), lies, urine marks, droppings etc. depending on animal's size. The calculation can be done for any unit of measurement (per 100 m or 1 km of the route, per 1 ha or 1 km^2) as well as depending on species and activity of the animal (and, correspondingly, on length of his movement).

The third possible characteristic is **food balance**. It is accepted to estimate the amount of eaten food per a unit of the route length or per unit of area. It is advised to count an approximate number of eaten plants (branches, trunk bark, cones and under-snow vegetation) for herbivorous animals, whereas for carnivores, a number and ration of successful and unsuccessful results of chasing. Number of droppings per unit of the route length or area also belongs to the food balance.

One more characteristic obtained from tracking can be ***biotopic*** (habitat – for small animals). It is advised to answer the following questions when analyzing tracking results: what habitats are preferable for the species, where it prefers to be fed, where it spends the night and where it spends the day.

When presenting all quantitative data, they should be in the form of a table. The following documents should be attached to the table: a map of the area where tracking has taken place (with tracking routes or without them), verbal description of habitats (preferable and "transitory" ones, verbal descriptions of non-standard behaviors that defy quantitative explanation: what pace an animal prefers, when and why speed of movement changes, how the animal marks its territory, how it treats individuals of the same species and individuals of different species, how it treats traces of man's activity and so on.

Physical and Chemical Properties of Natural Waters

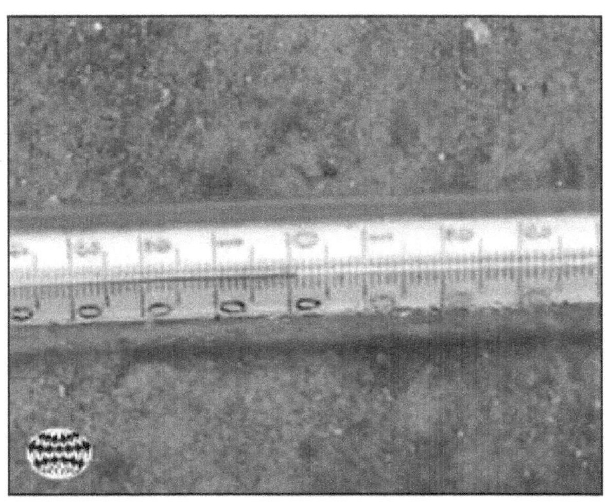

This manual contains guidelines for sampling natural and artificial bodies of water and snow sampling. It describes the procedure for determining the main physical properties of water including temperature, transparency, coloration, smell and total content of dredge and suspended particles. Quantitative analyses include acid estimation and oxygen content.

Introduction

Natural water contains many components that are found in low (less than 1%) and ultra-low (less than 1 one part per million) concentrations. In Russia, the state system of monitoring carries out the monitoring of natural and drinking water quality according to more than 50 parameters. In order to insure that water quality complies with special requirements, monitoring is carried out according to 100 or more components; many of them amount to one billionth and trillionth of a toxic substance (micrograms and nanograms of the substance per 1 liter of water). Certainly, such analyses are based on the application of modern and expensive equipment as well as the high qualifications of an analyst.

This manual focuses on only the **simplest parameters**; their determination will allow students to make a preliminary conclusion on water quality and characterize the purity of the water body.

This educational activity is aimed at water sampling from as **many water sources as possible** found within the vicinity of the school or field center as well as at comparison of some of the simplest physical and chemical properties of water taken from those sources.

Empty plastic bottles with screw-caps (one bottle per each water source), a shovel or a scoop, a glass cylinder about 50 cm high, different test-kits for determining water properties and clean plastic bags are required for this assignment.

Sampling

Sampling sites

When carrying out the given work, students should try to take water from a maximum number of sources in the area – both from natural water bodies and artificial ones. Water can be taken from local streams, rivers, lakes, ponds and water reservoirs (depending on their availability in the area) as well as from wells, water pipes, rainwater barrels, garden pools, etc. Snow samples should also be taken.

General rules of water sampling

Water sampling is an important part of water analysis and a necessary requirement for the reliability of obtained results and their applicability in practice. Mistakes arising from improper water sampling cannot be corrected later.

There are a number of general rules of water sampling for further analyses regardless of the source of water samples.

1) **A standard type of container** should be used as jars for all water sampling. At present it is more convenient to use clear 1-2-litre

bottled water plastic bottles for these purposes. They should be washed beforehand without use of detergents and then dried out.

2) Prior to water sampling, the bottle should be **rinsed several times** with the water under study.

3) The bottle should be **filled with water up to the very top** and the cap should be screwed so that there is absolutely no air left in the bottle.

4) In all water sources, the bottle should be **immersed into water completely** (with the exception of a faucet). It should be placed 10 cm lower the water surface so that water surface film does not go into the bottle.

5) When sampling water, it is necessary to **measure water temperature** regardless of the water source. Temperature can be taken with the help of a regular thermometer, which should be immersed into water for a minute. The temperature should be read without taking the thermometer out of the water. When sampling water running from the faucet, the head of a thermometer is placed into the water current right at the faucet outlet.

6) Each bottle containing a water sample should be **labeled immediately** at the sampling site. Students must also record details of the water sampling in their field notebooks. It is sufficient to write down the name of the water source and the number of the sample on the bottle in indelible marker. It is advised to write prior to sampling, when the bottle is dry. More detailed information is taken down in the field notebook. It usually includes the following standard data: the number of the water sample, the date, time and authors of the sample, geographical and local position of the sampling site (region, district, human settlement, name of the water body, position of the site in relation to other landmarks and so on (more details – the better). The method of water sampling should also be described (from a bank, from a boat, from a bridge, out of a well-bucket, from under a faucet, etc.), as well as water temperature at the moment of sampling.

7) After a sample has been taken, it is necessary to observe the **basic rules of sample storage**: it is advised to carry out the main analyses in the course of an hour from the moment of sampling (especially analyses of smell, transparency and oxygen content (if

needed). Other parameters can be determined in the days after samples have been taken. If determination of water properties cannot be conducted at once, the sample should be preserved (each component or a group of substances is characterized with an independent procedure for preservation) or stored in the refrigerator at a temperature of 3-4 degrees Celsius no longer than 3-5 days.

Techniques of water-sampling

Two techniques of water sampling are applied in environmental monitoring: one-time and multiple. In case of a **one-time sampling**, the water sample is taken once in a certain place. However, one-time water sampling is not enough for valid conclusions on the state of the water body, as in most cases water quality varies in different locations within the same water-body and in different seasons. Nevertheless, conditions of the given educational activity do not allow to take samples many times, i.e. do not involve serial sampling. However, information how it can be done can be useful for students, thus, it is given in a footnote.

When conducting **multiple sampling**, each sample is taken in specific relation to all the other ones. **Zonal sampling** can serve as a typical example. While carrying out **zonal sampling**, samples are taken at different depths along a chosen range (line) of a water reservoir, a lake or a river. A series of samples are usually taken for determination of seasonal or diurnal changes in water properties. Sampling should be carried out taking into account hydrological season (flood or low-water period) when defining seasonal changes.

So-called **matched samples** represent a specific type of serial (multiple) sampling. The samples are taken in different locations along the river's stream current taking into account water flow-through time. A fishing float can be used as a control, it is sent downstream in order to control water flow from one point to another. Source of pollution or a wastewater discharge points can easily be found out in the course of such sampling.

Averaged sample of flowing water is taken at places with the strongest current.

Sampling in water-bodies

A site for water sampling at the water body is chosen according to a preliminary study of the area. All conditions (season, precipitation, location of potential and known sources of pollution, etc.) that can influence the composition of the sample should be taken into consideration. It is necessary to pay special attention to the **presence of tributaries and sources of river basin pollution**, which may be located upstream of the sampling site. All of the aforementioned conditions can influence the results of analyses and will help then to explain revealed differences among water sources.

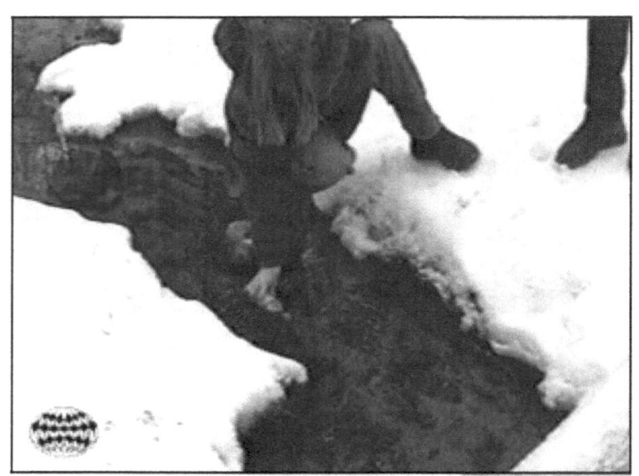

Students should be governed by the following **rules when selecting a specific site** for water sampling at water bodies:

1) Water sampling should be conducted at typical, meaning average in all respects, water body segments – at a section of open water, if possible, with an average current and at sites of average depth.

2)   It is advised to **avoid taking samples of stagnant water** in front of dams, in river bends, in dead river branches, etc. In particular, obvious, polluted, stagnant places should be avoided.

Snow sampling

Snow sampling is not a primary activity of this lesson, it is used only for the comparison of the physical and chemical composition of melting water with other water sources in the vicinity of the school or field study center. However, analysis of snow properties can be quite interesting in itself, as it can provide much toward an understanding of air pollution conditions in the given area.

Snow, which have fallen in winter, accumulates many pollutants which precipitate from air and are contained in snow itself. Snow represents peculiar chemical chronicles of the winter. Snow cover pollution can be determined independently with the help of the procedure for complete snow survey or snow survey along a landscape profile (see Lesson #10, winter) with subsequent analysis of taken samples according to main parameters. At the same time students can make a **map** of snow cover pollution and find out main air pollution **sources**, as well as to determine degree and frontiers of their impact. It is easier to reveal such sources of pollutants as boilers, motor transport, plants and factories belonging to heavy and energy industries.

There are peculiarities in the procedure for snow sampling for the purposes of physical and chemical analyses. Three snow samples should be taken at the same place in order to obtain valid data. It is done as follows:

1)   A **site for snow sampling** is chosen so that it is possible to plot a triangle on it, and its sides should be not less than 10 m long (10-30 m).

2) **Squares one meter to a side** should be marked off at vertices of the plotted triangle, so we end up with three such squares.

3) The snow is taken with the help of **"an envelope" technique** in these squares, i.e. samples are taken in the corners of the square (four samples) and in the center of the square. All together, five samples are taken from each square, and all the samples are combined and used for one analysis. So three squares in the vertices of a triangle make up 15 samples, i.e. in five samples for each separate analysis.

4) Snow is taken from almost the **whole depth of the snow cover**. This is done in order to summarize all the pollution accumulated in the snow during winter. The snow is sampled either with a cylinder, a shovel or a scoop.

All fifteen samples are put into a clean plastic bag. Students should bear in mind that snow volume should be rather big; taking into

account the fact that when snow melts its volume will reduce approximately 10 times. So if you have to obtain, for instance, 1 liter of melt water, you have to collect about 10 liters of snow (about a bucket).

Snow can be taken barehanded (make sure that your hands are clean), but students should avoid touching the inner surface of the plastic bag. The plastic bag with snow is tied and packed into the second bag. A piece of paper with sample description and its marking label should be put into the second plastic bag. Plastic bags can be stored in the refrigerator or on the porch.

Prior to analyses, the snow from the plastic bag should be melted and warmed to room temperature. If the bag is waterproof, it is enough just to put the bag in a warm room and leave it there for 2-3 hours, or to take the snow out into a clean enamel basin or into a bucket.

Determination of general physical and chemical properties of water

The main physical parameters measured are temperature, smell, transparency (optical transmission) and coloration. Determination of the content of suspended particles and solutes require some simple equipment.

The **main chemical parameters** that can be measured depend on availability of equipment, reagents or test-kits for analyses of water properties at the school or field study center.

At minimum, an optimal case includes analyses of the following water properties: acidity (pH), total or carbonate water hardness, contents of nitrates or ammonium. It is more interesting (and more expensive) to obtain data on the content of dissolved oxygen, carbon dioxide, iron and phenols. Nevertheless, most analyses can be made with the use of test-kits that are in stores. Let us focus on the procedures of the simplest analyses.

Temperature

As mentioned above, temperature measurement at water sampling is an integral part of the analysis. Temperature should be taken again prior to the main analyses in the laboratory. Large differences in temperature can have an influence upon some results, for instance, pH.

Transparency (optical transmission)

Water transparency depends on **water coloration and turbidity**. Water transparency can be measured at the sampling site with the help of a so-called Sekki disc. It is a white disk 30 cm in diameter (for

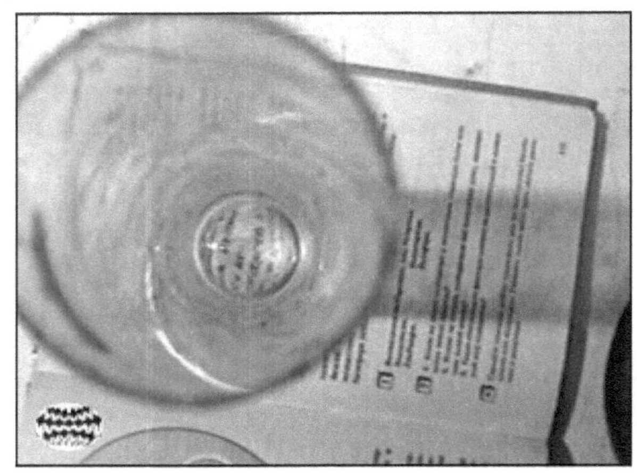

instance, the white cover of an enamel bucket), which is sunk on a rope into the water from a boat or a bridge. The depth where the disk disappears is measured and taken for a relative value of water transparency. However, although this technique it is a professional method, is labor-intensive and not always available, so we recommend another technique for the given educational purposes – with the help of printing type.

A glass cylinder measuring 40-60 cm tall (usually available with chemical laboratory glassware) is used for determining water transparency. It is placed on a qualitative printing type of a standard size - 3.5 mm (for instance on a book page) in the laboratory at normal room lighting. Then the water under study is slowly poured into the cylinder while a student looks at the printing type from above, through the column of poured water. Water is added to the cylinder until the letters become blurred and the text is not readable. This height is taken for water transparency. Again as in the case with measurement of water transparency using the **Sekki disc**, the obtained value is a relative parameter, meaning that the results can be compared with other results only if they have been obtained with the help of the same procedure.

Both above-described procedures for determination of water transparency are widely accepted as standard. In the first case, water transparency is measured in meters, in the second case – in centimeters.

Data on water transparency indicate not only the degree of saturation of water with suspended particles, but the depth of sunlight penetration into the body of water as well.

Coloration

Water color is determined simultaneously as the measurement of water transparency.

Professional hydrologists and hydrochemists determine water color in field conditions with the help of a color scale consisting of 22 glass test-tubes filled with color solutions of different tints from blue to brown. In order to determine water color with the help of the mentioned technique, a Sekki disc is immersed into water at the depth equal to half of the transparency value. Then the water color against the white disc is compared to the color of the solutions in test-tubes. A color is determined and marked with the number of the corresponding test-tube.

A simple technique, but not as precise as the previous one, is suggested for the purposes of this educational activity, using the same glass cylinder, which has been used for measurement of water transparency. Before the water is poured out of the cylinder, it is placed on a piece of white paper and the **color of the water inside the cylinder is defined visually**. Water color is described according to the following standard scale: colorless, blue, green, yellow-green, green-yellow, yellow, brownish yellow, light brown, fulvous (dull brown/tawny). Turbid water should be drained prior to determination of its color. Ideally if there is another glass cylinder available, it can be filled with distilled water or pure absolutely colorless water for comparison.

Smell

Water smell is caused by **volatile odorous substances**, which come into water naturally or with wastewater. Wastewater pollution is revealed not only according to their smell, but also according to the smell of the products of their decomposing components.

Some types of aquatic organisms have specific smells, which resemble, for instance, smell of *cucumber (Synura), violets (Mallomonas), pigsty (Anabaena)* and so on.

The smell of wastewater coming from human settlements is a mixture of feces odor with smells of soap, grease, and putrefaction (hydrogen sulfide), and is quite distinctive. Wastewater coming from coal thermal treatment is characterized with a smell of phenols (distinct heavy pharmaceutical smell), resins, hydrogen sulfide, etc.

Water smell is determined at **20 and 60 degrees Celsius**. The smell is described verbally, for instance, "earthy", "fecal", "putrid", "grassy", "moldy", "musty." The smell of chemical substances might be described as "phenol", "resinous", " organic solvent", "iodine", etc. Determination of smell intensity and nature depends on experience and the individual abilities of the researcher, so it is advised to determine the nature of the smell collectively in order to avoid subjective estimations.

The **technical procedure for smell determination** is as follows: 250 ml of water is poured into a flask at 20 degrees Celsius. The flask is capped and its contents are thoroughly shaken several times. Then the flask is opened and smell should be determined immediately. Another flask is warmed in a water bath (or in a drying oven) up to 60 degrees Celsius. The neck of the flask should be covered with a watch crystal. Flask contents are stirred and the smell and its intensity are determined immediately.

Smell intensity is determined by dilution of the sample with distilled water until smell disappears.

Total content of suspended particles and solutes

All substances found in water can be divided into **suspended particles** and **solutes**. In practice, determination of suspended particles consists of water filtration, subsequent drying of a filter and its accurate weighing. The procedure for determination of solute content consists in evaporation of strained water and the subsequent

weighing of evaporated residuum.

This task should be performed in the course of this activity only in case if an analytical balance, a drying oven and filters for quantitative determination are available at the school or field study center.

Prior to work, one or two paper filters out of a bundle of filters are checked. Each dried and weighted filter is rinsed with 100 ml of distilled water and then it is dried and weighted again. The loss in weight should be not more than 10% of the filter's weight.

Each filter should be dried and weighed before use. Then a volume of mixed sample (100 – 500 ml depending on the purity of water) is measured off and filtered through a funnel. The filter with filter cake is dried first in air and then in a drying oven to its constant weight at a temperature equal to 105 degrees Celsius. Then the filter is weighed. The amount of suspended particles in the sample is calculated according to the weight difference of a dried filter before and after use. Then the content of suspended substances is estimated per a unit of water volume (g/l).

Determination of snow contamination according to the amount of dust particles (suspended particles) is of particular interest when precision analytical balance is not available. This procedure is considerably simpler than the study of natural water with low concentration of dredge, though it is similar to the above-described process. Melt water, which is obtained from snow samples, is thoroughly mixed and poured through a weighed dry paper filter (it is advised to filter not less than 1 liter of water through it). A filter with filter cake consisting of suspended particles is dried in a drying oven and then weighed. Studies of snow can result in making a map of snow cover pollution in the vicinity of the school, and if taking into account a wind rose, it is possible to discover the main plants that pollute the environment and to prove transport contribution to environmental pollution.

Solutes are determined by evaporation of an already strained water sample. First it is necessary to weigh a porcelain cup, then an appropriate amount of filtered water is poured into the cup and its contents are evaporated in a drying oven.

If total mineralization exceeds 5 g/l, then solute can be detected with the help of procedures of qualitative analysis. If mineralization is less than 5 g/l it is useless to make a qualitative analysis in school laboratory conditions.

Some qualitative chemical analyses

Qualitative determination (i.e. determination of the presence or absence of a substance in the sample) of some of the most widespread solute admixtures is carried out with the help of following reaction.

Determination of nitrates

Nitrates are found almost in all types of waters. A large content of nitrates indicates past pollution with sewage (fecal) waters. The determination of nitrates in underground waters serves as an evaluation of mineralization when water is drained through soil layers. When studying surface waters, the presence of nitrates can serve as an indicator of **waste nitrification**. Violations of mineral fertilizer application procedures can serve as a source of nitrates in areas of intensive agricultural development.

The following analyses are made in order to determine the presence of nitrates in water. Two ml of a test sample is dropped into 5 ml of concentrated sulfuric acid in a test-tube that is constantly stirred. Then a very small amount of solid brucine (careful, it is a powerful poison!) is added and the mixture is stirred again. A resulting yellow or mahogany coloration indicates the presence of nitrates. Sensitivity of the reaction is 1 mg/l and higher.

Determination of sulfates

The presence of sulfates – salts of sulfuric acid - can be increased in water bodies due to **discharge of wastewater** containing inorganic and organic sulfur compounds.

The following procedure is used for determining the presence of sulfates. Approximately 10 ml of the water sample is acidified in a test-tube with several drops of hydrochloric acid and then about 0.5 ml of 10% solution of barium chloride ($BaCl_2$) or barium nitrate ($BaNO_3$) is added to the mixture.

If sulfate content is about 5-50 mg/l, then a slight turbidity appears. If the concentration of sulfates is higher, then precipitate of barium sulfate (nitrate) BaSO4 falls out.

Iron determination

Iron salts are present in **surface and ground waters** – their natural concentration depends on geological structure and hydrological conditions of the river basin. High iron content in surface waters indicates water pollution with industrial or mine wastewater, especially wastewater coming from metalworking plants, etching works, etc.

The presence of iron in water can be determined with the help of two procedures that require adding reagents to the water sample and analysis of an evaporated residuum. In the first case, 10 ml of a water sample is poured into a test-tube, then one drop of aquafortis (concentrated nitric acid), several drops of 5% solution of hydrogen peroxide and about 0.5 ml of 20% solution of potassium thiocyanate are added. If iron content is about 0.1 mg/l then a light pink coloration of the solution will appear. If iron content in water sample is higher, a red color will appear.

The other procedure is as follows: If a dry yellow or light yellow residuum is left in the cup after water evaporation, then iron salts can be discovered with the help of solutions of potassium ferricyanide as well as potassium or ammonium thiocyanate. The appearance of blue residuum caused by potassium ferricyanide as well as a blood red color caused by ammonium thiocyanate indicates presence of iron ions.

Chlorides (salts of hydrochloric acid) are detected according to water cloudiness when adding silver nitrate or lead nitrate (0.1 mole/l) with subsequent cooling of the test-tube under a stream of cold water.

It is advised to determine **hydrocarbonates** (acid salts of carbonic acid) if the pH of the test water sample is equal or more than 7. A solution of hydrochloric acid is added drop by drop to the test water sample. An intensive, odorless bubbling indicates the presence of hydrocarbonates.

If the solution of hydrochloric acid is added to the residuum that has been cooled after evaporation, and boiling with bubble-formation is observed, this means that it is hydrocarbonate water. If the solution does not boil, it means that it contains calcium or magnesium sulfates and chlorides.

If water tastes salty or bitter/salty then dry residuum can be analyzed for the presence of sodium or potassium salts. It can be done as follows: Put some dry residuum on a tip of a knife made of stainless steel and then bring it into an outer cone of torch flame. A yellow flame indicates the presence of **sodium salts**, whereas a lilac-violet color will reveal presence of **potassium salts**, and a brick-red color, the presence of **calcium salts**.

Determination of phenols

Phenols are aromatic chemical compounds with one or several hydroxyl groups attached directly to a benzene ring, for instance, *phenol, cresols, thymol, chlorophenols and nitrophenols*. If their concentration is about several milligrams per 1 liter, they can exert influence upon the biological life of water bodies. Some phenols (if their concentration is about several micrograms per 1 liter) cause objectionable chlorophenol odor and taste, which appears after chlorination of surface waters in the course of drinking water disinfection.

In order to detect the presence of phenols in water, 100 ml of a test sample is poured into a beaker flask of 200 ml and then a solution of bleaching powder or chlorine water is added to the sample so that 0.05 mg of active chlorine is added. A characteristic "pharmaceutical" smell of chlorophenols is checked in 10 minutes at 20 and 60 degrees Celsius (see procedure of smell determination).

Some quantitative chemical analyses

Any quantitative chemical analyses, i.e. analyses that produce data on content (quantity) of a chemical substance in water, require expensive equipment, chemical knowledge, accuracy in test procedure compliance. Therefore, they can be performed by students only in conditions of a **well-equipped chemical laboratory** under supervision of a chemistry teacher. Thus, at the present lesson we recommend not to go deep into qualitative measurements, but to use numerous test-kits that allow you to determine roughly both qualitative and some quantitative properties of water. First of all, they include such parameters as acidity (pH), and the concentration of

nitrates, ammonium, oxygen and carbon dioxide.

Test-kits for all mentioned substances are sold at aquarium supply stores. We will briefly describe most widespread chemical analyses of great importance in ecological studies in the given section.

Water acidity (content of hydrogen ions or pH)

Acidity or pH of water indicates whether it is acidic or alkaline water, and is measured in the range of 0 to 14. The value of 7 is neutral according to scale of acidity, from 6 to 0 – acidic, and from 8 to 15 – alkaline.

Stagnant (swamp) water is usually acidic (4 - 5) due to the presence of organic acids, whereas normal clean water has pH value close to neutral (6.5 – 8.5). It is accepted that pH values from 5.5. to 8.5 are optimal for development of aquatic organisms.

An abrupt change of pH in a water body can lead to the dilution of some substances in water and poisoning of aquatic organisms. If pH values suddenly change and become more acidic or alkaline, special attention should be paid to possible industrial discharge.

As far as precipitation acidity concerns, clean rainwater and clean snow have pH value 5.6 – it is slightly more acid than the pH value of distilled water (pH=7). It happens as easily soluble carbon dioxide is always present in air.

When it combines with water, it forms carbonic acid, which acidifies atmospheric precipitates. If there are many nitrogen oxides, sulfur dioxide (SO_4) and other acidic substances present in the air, then pH values of snow or rainwater will be less than 5.6. If the pH value of snow is higher than 5.6 then it is alkaline and it is most likely polluted with metal oxides and/or automobile exhaust gases (aromatic hydrocarbons).

It is easier to determine pH with the help of indicator bands with different measuring ranges, which are produced in many countries. However, this method is the least accurate one of all the test methods; its accuracy is 0.5 - 1.

Liquid test-kits provide best results, where several drops of a chemical reagent are added to the test water sample, and the water color obtained is compared to the provided color scale. The accuracy of such tests is up to 0.2 – 0.5.

Determination of dissolved oxygen

Dissolved oxygen content is one of the most important biological properties of water as it indicates the presence of organic substances in water and serves as an evidence of respiration and decay in the body of water.

Low oxygen content indicates a large inflow of organic substances into water, for instance, from stock-farms or sewage discharge. Oxygen content in water also depends on water temperature. It has also been revealed that the oxygen content in water is dependent upon photosynthesis. The more plants that are found in water, the higher the oxygen content during daylight time, while less at night. Considerable diurnal variation is registered, which also has to be taken into account when taking water samples.

The European Commission on Environmental Conservation set the maximum acceptable level of dissolved oxygen content as 4 mg/l.

Indices below the mentioned value indicate pollution of the water body.

As for most qualitative analyses, the simplest method of oxygen content measurement is an analysis with the help of test-kits or an instrument called an oxygen-meter.

Presentation of results

This activity should result in a table of comparative data on water properties in different natural water bodies, artificial water sources and properties of snow in the vicinity of the school or field study center. The number of studied parameters and sources is not regulated according to the given educational task, as it depends on availability of test-kits, equipment and chemical reagents, as well as on the presence of water sources.

Results obtained for different sources should be compared and students should try to reveal the causes of found differences: why a specific water-body is characterized with specific properties of water. What determines snow and rainwater properties in different locations?

If any material resources (test-kits, chemical reagents and instruments) are lacking, the activity can be focused on analysis of physical properties of water taken from different sources (the more, the better) and on making a map of snow cover pollution with suspended particles.

Study of Snow Cover Profile

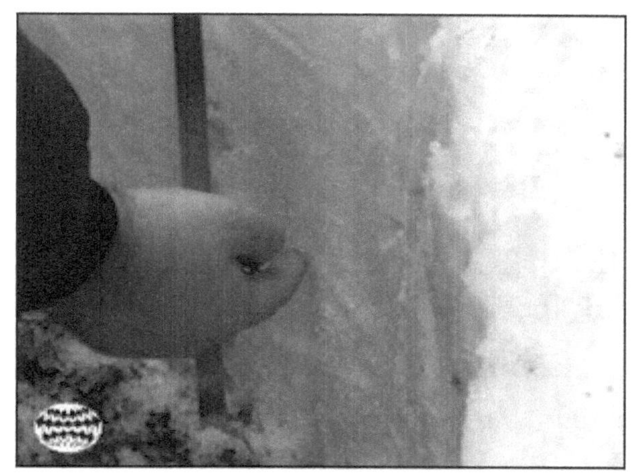

This manual describes the main functions and features of snow cover, and a procedure for snow survey along a landscape profile. The activity includes location of survey sites, establishment of snow exploring shaft, determination of snow layers according to a number of visual characteristics, their measurement and description.

Introduction

One of the most important landscape characteristics in winter are the **properties of snow cover** – its thickness and density, as well as depth of the frost zone at different sites. It is well known that preservation of seeds and sprouts from winterkill as well as the wintering success of many animal species depends on the depth of the soil frost zone.

Depth of the seasonal frost zone is of great importance, as it influences peculiarities of spring soil erosion causing destruction of soil structure. Unfortunately, the study of permafrost is complicated by its laboriousness and use of specific equipment, for example, the soil probe. Thus, this educational activity will be focused on snow –

i.e. peculiarities of its distribution along the relief forms and under different vegetation types, structure of snow cover and study of snow's role in landscape function.

The activity is aimed at revealing the **dependence** of the thickness and structure of snow cover upon **relief forms** and **vegetation type**. It is known that snow cover is thinner and distributed unevenly in coniferous forests.

In contrast, the distribution of snow in deciduous forests is thicker and more evenly distributed. In comparing a forest and an open site, it turns out that wind is much lighter in forests than in open areas, so snow is not blown off the soil surface. Thus, snow cover in forests is characterized by a more even distribution than in the field, for instance, where wind differentiates thickness of the snow cover by stripping rises and filling up relief depressions with snow.

In order to complete the task, students will require shovels (for unearthing snow), rulers (it is recommended to use long rulers – for the full depth of the snow cover) or measuring tapes, description forms (soil description forms can be used) or field logs, compasses and some other materials at hand (sticks, blades and matches).

The teacher should explain the main functions and properties of the snow cover before the activities, and students should be taught how to measure and describe the snow cover prior to independent studies.

Main functions of snow cover

The role of snow in the function of an environment is especially obvious when air temperature falls below zero degrees centigrade. In areas where there is no snow in cold seasons, soil gets frozen through for many meters, and, for instance, in Yakutia, the depth of permafrost makes up one and a half kilometer.

The preservative function of snow or **thermal insulation** is, perhaps, the most important one. It is known that snow cover has loose structure due to the different shapes of snowflakes. Interstices among snowflakes are filled up with air that is characterized by *low heat conductivity*, so we owe such a wonderful property of snow to

air. The air, as we sometimes (but incorrectly) say, "warms up well."

Due to the low heat conductivity of snow, day-to-day temperature variation penetrates into the snow cover only for a depth of 24 centimeters on average. As specific research has shown, if the amplitude of temperature fluctuation reaches 30 degrees at the snow surface, then at 5 cm depth it amounts to only 16 degrees, at 24 cm depth it makes up 3 degrees and at 44 cm depth the amplitude is insignificant – 0.8 degrees.

Not just soils are protected from frost penetration due to snow as mentioned above, but plants as well, which can stay green through the winter. They often serve as the only food for animals, and harbor seeds, which serve as security for renewal of the vegetation cover in spring.

However, snow is known not only for its heat insulating function. As snow is water in solid aggregative state, it **accumulates** in large quantities and remains until spring in order to water the earth and allow plants to start growing when it becomes warm.

Besides heat insulating and accumulating functions, snow cover also exerts **influence upon a climate.**

Everyone knows that air masses move around the earth's surface. Coming from remote areas, they bring along characteristics of the area they originated from – mainly air **humidity** and **temperature**. As they move above the surface continuously, they change slightly; however, if they stagnate in one area for a certain time, they acquire temperature and moisture characteristics of the given region.

It is also known that air cannot be heated directly by the sun. Sunlight is absorbed by a surface and then the surface gives heat back to the air in the form of infrared radiation. Some solar radiation is reflected by the surface in the form of light and is not transformed into heat. The less is the surface reflection power and the higher its absorption capacity, the warmer the surface becomes. Thus, surface temperature depends on its reflection properties, or *albedo*.

The albedo of a black body is equal to 0%, whereas the albedo of a white body is equal to 100%. Fresh-fallen snow is very close to 100% according to its albedo. Correspondingly, when the ground is covered with snow, the ground cannot warm up air anymore. So, air is cooled. Hence, winter temperature conditions are partly kept by this phenomenon. So if, at last, the sun peeps out and one would think it can become warmer, it does not happen. Spring and the corresponding rise in temperature are brought by warm air masses that have been warmed up in other regions of the Earth, which are not covered with snow.

One more significant characteristic of snow is that snow **clears the atmosphere** from mechanical and chemical pollution. Smog over a city, which consists of acid deposition, exhaust gases, aerosols and radionuclids in different forms, disappears after a snowfall. However, this fact does not make plants happy, as melting snow gives all absorbed pollutants back to the soil in spring.

Main properties of snow cover

Structure of snow cover is characterized by such significant properties (values) as **thickness** and **density**, which are closely interrelated. They depend on a number of factors, including amount of precipitation, temperature conditions, peculiarities of relief and vegetation.

Thickness of the snow cover grows in the course of winter and it reaches its maximum value in March (in regions in Central Russia). The snow depth could be maximum too, if it did not compact under the influence of thaws, its own gravity force and other reasons.

Snow is greatly intertwined and compacted under the influence of a wind at open sites, thus there is little snow left in some places and high snowdrifts are formed in others. The wind loses its power within forests and it barely shifts snow masses. However, even within the

forest, snow cover is uneven, but due to other reasons. Most snow is accumulated at forest glades and in open spaces among trees, in desolated roads and paths. The shallowest depth of snow is found around tree trunks as thick snowflakes remain on tree branches and form a "snow overhang" or "*kukhta*", which becomes bigger from one snowfall till another, especially when it is calm. Kukhta can become very large in some geographical regions. Coniferous trees in forests in the middle Urals get covered with such a strong shell made of frozen snow that it is difficult to break it with a stick. Thick kukhta covers lower branches of spruce up to three and more meters high completely in March.

Due to formation of even thinner kukhta than in the Urals there is less snow under the forest canopy and it is distributed unevenly. More snow is found in deciduous forests, considerably less snow is characteristic of pine forests and especially little snow is registered in spruce, fir and cedar dark-coniferous forests.

Initial density of the snow cover depends on weather conditions when the snow falls and, consequently, on the form of falling snowflakes. Snowflakes represent compound multifaceted stars in calm weather and light frost. Such snowflakes easily grapple with each other, forming loose flakes, which fall down slowly and quietly and create a fluffy shroud. Much air remains among the facets of snowflakes and because of this, snow obtains its blinding whiteness that is characteristic of fresh-fallen snow. However, snowflakes lose their facets in the course of time due to the effects of their own gravity force as well as other reasons. They turn into simple ice crystals that fit closer and closer together so that the snow gradually gets compacted.

Snow density and, primarily, density of the top snow layer is intensively influenced by a strong wind. It is clear that **wind's greatest influence** is exerted in open spaces – in fields, vast swamps and large water bodies. There, compact crust is quite often formed on the surface of snow cover; it is also called "a wind board."

The role of wind is considerably smaller in forests, not taking into account certain sites that border windward forest edges. Snow is compacted under the influence of its own weight in temperature differences in forests, whereas under tree crowns it is rammed by the heavy weight of falling kukhta.

Snow density becomes greater under the influence of all the above-mentioned factors; the snow is more intensively compacted at the end of winter and in early spring.

Snow gradually loses its initial whiteness in the course of time; moreover, it gets littered even in dense forests far from any human settlements and busy roads with their smoke and ash. It gets littered with old needles, small twigs, seeds and other natural forest debris.

When snow falls in hard frost and with a strong wind, then we observe not the above-mentioned compound stars but ice crystals and even needles which prick our faces so painfully in snowstorms. Such snowflakes fall down, fit together tightly and immediately form a compact snow cover.

Ice crusts that differ in thickness, compactness and located at different depths are formed as a result of temperature drops, which are quite often registered before winter and in the course of winter months when thaws are replaced by frost. Some ice crusts appear on the threshold of winter close to the ground surface or surround and "lock" the ground herbage. They are called "ground-glass" and cause many difficulties to wintering animals as they prevent animals from getting food, digging snow, and moving freely in snow.

Ice crusts are quite often formed on the snow surface itself, in the form of a thin crust of ice over snow. If this thin crust is then covered with a layer of fresh-fallen snow and it is repeated several times during winter, then buried ice crusts appear within the snow cover.

Besides formation of different ice crusts, the structure of snow, especially its lower layers, undergoes great changes and obtains a *macrocrystalline structure* in the course of time.

Snow Survey at the Profile

Organization of field activities

Optimal organization of training activities within the framework of the given educational task is to have students work at the same site where a slope profile has been established (Lesson #3, fall) and soil and geobotanical studies have taken place (Lesson # 8, fall).

In any case, it is recommended to study snow cover at a section of the river (stream) valley slope where **different relief types** are represented, including depressions around the river-bed, floodplain,

terraces (flat areas in the lower course of macrorelief), watershed (a flat area located at a certain eminence), slopes of different steepness, as well as **different plant associations** including a meadow association, a deciduous forest, a mixed forest, a pine and a spruce forest (ideally).

It is convenient when a length of the profile is not large – from 200 m up to 1 km. It will be easier to organize activities of different teams at such a section.

A group of students consisting of 10-15 people is divided into teams of two. Each team is given a task to describe a number of certain points along the profile. Selection of points (description sites) is determined by a number of student teams and the diversity of conditions along the profile line. Description should cover all the present diversity of relief forms and vegetation types; in addition, it is advised to make descriptions under different conditions – for instance, under the tree crown and at a certain distance away from the tree, for instance, in the clearing. However, it is not necessary to carry out the descriptions in such pairs everywhere – it is enough to make two such descriptions in each forest type (under a birch and in the clearing within the birch forest, under a pine and in the clearing in stand of pine trees, under a spruce and in the clearing within the spruce forest, etc.)

Description of snow cover

A **Snow pit** is established at a site in order to describe the snow cover. This is a pit in the snow, of a size large enough so that it is possible to get into the snow pit without destroying of the snow pit wall (usually 1.5 m x 1.5 m). The snow pit is dug with a shovel for the whole depth of the snow cover – to the ground below. Unlike a soil pit, the wall of the snow pit should not be located facing the sun. Even in frosty weather, the sun can quickly warm up snow and it will change the picture for the description of snow features.

The snow from the pit should also be put at one of the sides as when digging a soil pit, the front wall (the wall prepared for description) should not be touched or stepped on and snow should not be put close to it.

When the snow pit is dug out, first topsoil vegetation should be described (before it is trampled down) – approximate plant composition is taken down (if there are green plants, they should be described separately) and their approximate numbers (projective percent of cover). Ground properties are determined together with a description of topsoil vegetation – whether it is frozen or not, then its **temperature** should be taken. If there is no soil thermometer, it can be done with a regular one. A small cavity in the ground is made with the help of a pen or a stick and the head of a regular thermometer is placed into the cavity for one minute. It is recommended to write down the temperature without taking the thermometer out of the ground. Choose a site for measuring ground temperature not in the middle of the study area (as ground changes its temperature very quickly there) but under the snow pit wall itself.

Measure the temperature **inside** the snow cover immediately before the description –place a thermometer into two or three loose layers at different depths for one minute. This data, together with temperature of the ground under the scow cover and air temperature (it can be measured at a person's height) will provide additional interesting information on heat-conducting properties of snow.

The next stage of field studies is **snow cover description** itself. The vertical front snow wall should be **smoothed out** – a thin layer of snow should be peeled off the whole depth of the shaft with a shovel edge – top-down so that the snow will be fresh and clean, immediately before the description. The front wall should be as even and vertical as possible.

The first stage of description is measurement of the **total thickness** of the snow cover. Snow cover depth is measured with a ruler (it is recommended to have long rulers, which will be long enough to measure the whole thickness of the snow) or a measuring tape.

Then students proceed with the most difficult stage of the description – determination of borders of snow horizons (layers). For this purpose, the front wall is closely examined and probed according to the following characteristics of each layer: color, graininess, moisture and density (hardness).

The **color** is determined visually according to the following four classes (in compliance with a standard): *white, white-gray, gray* and *bluish gray*.

Three gradations are defined according to structure of the snow (**graininess**): *fine-grain, medium-grained* and *coarse-grained* snow.

Two gradations are determined in accordance with **moisture**: a *dry* snow – which forms fragile snowballs, pours off the shovel and is usually loose and friable; and *wet* – which forms sticky, firm snowballs that are easily made, and can form snow blocks.

Four gradations of snow are defined according to **density** (solidity): *fresh-fallen* (very soft), *packed* (soft), *compacted* (hard) and *solid* (very hard). Snow density can be measured the following way: four fingers easily penetrate into very soft snow, only one finger can penetrate into soft snow, whereas hard snow can be permeated only by a pencil, and very hard snow – only by a knife. Granulated snow (firn) and ice are described separately when determining density of snow cover. Firn is an intermediate state between snow and ice – it consists of compacted grains of ice, but it is not yet ice.

Layers of snow cover are first determined visually (defining their color and graininess) and by moving a fingertip gently along the snow wall (upwards) trying to feel changes in density and structure of snow layers. Change in any of above-described properties of snow is an indicator of a layer border. To make the following measurements easier it is possible to mark borders between snow layers by putting objects into the snow – twigs, blades of grass, matches.

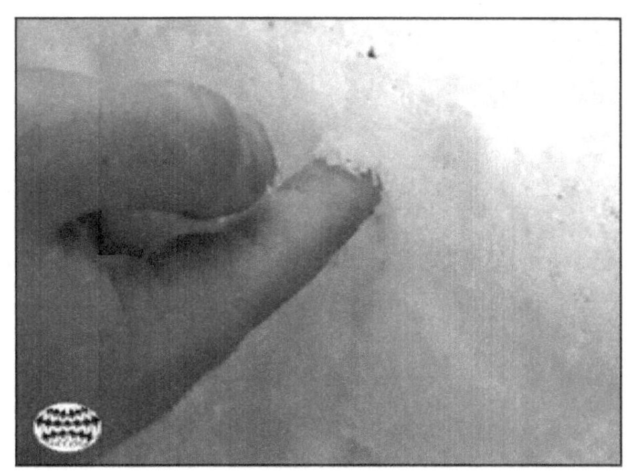

When determining the density of snow, i.e. moving a fingertip along the wall, it is necessary to note presence of thin crusts of ice (on the snow surface), ice streaks within the snow cover – buried crusts as well as the presence of ice on the surface of ground or herbage (ground crust). Such crusts are also recorded, even though they can be very thin (sometimes they are less than 1 mm thick).

The next stage is measuring the thickness of each layer and their description.

To make the description easier it is possible to use **forms** that are similar to forms of soil profile description (or use those forms instead, see lesson #4, fall). It is also possible not to go beyond drawing of schemes in the field diary.

In any case it is suggested to **plot borders between snow layers** on the scheme (which are measured with the help of a ruler) upwards – where ground surface is taken for zero (start). The thickness of each layer (it is measured directly or calculated later according to a scheme) and its properties should be drawn and described on the scheme of snow cover structure. Similar to a description of soil horizons, verbal descriptions of each snow layer should be given by hand on the right of the drawing, opposite the given layer on the scheme.

The concluding stage of field description is **associated data**. Similar to soil description, associated data includes the date, time and authors of the description, geographical and local situation (region, area, human settlement and so on), position of the snow shaft (its location in relief, within the landscape profile; it is recommended to write down direction of the slope relative to North and South if possible), description of surrounding tree-and-shrubby vegetation (name of the plant association, formula of the forest stand, density of crowns and height of trees) as well as peculiarities of the given snow shaft (under a tree, at a glade, with its distance to the closest tree, etc.) The more small details of the snow shaft location recorded the better.

Lab studies of materials

When students come back to the laboratory, they should collect and arrange all descriptions made during field studies. This should result in a drawing of the landscape profile (a relief line) with shown conventions of the snow cover properties.

The first stage is **unification** of the description. It consists of the detection of certain common properties of all described snow pits – for instance, presence of the same number of main layers (usually there are only three to five layers which are parted by ice crusts). At this stage the teacher should analyze independent studies of students and check that there are not too many layers found (sometimes it is possible to count more layers than there are, due to

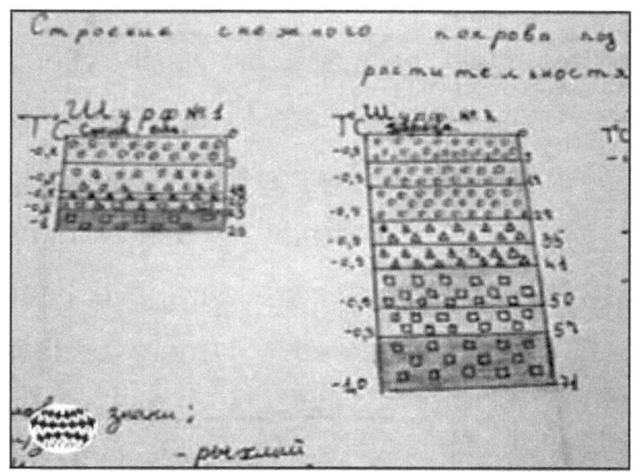

excessive eagerness of some students) or – on the contrary – too little. It is suggested that the teacher should check several description sites in order to make description results reliable.

Then a system of **conventions** should be developed. They are mainly applied to a pictorial rendition of graininess and density of snow layers. Snow density is usually expressed with the help of color: the denser the layer, the darker the color.

Different tints of the color are used: from light blue in case of fresh-fallen, very soft snow to dark blue in case of firm snow and black – for ice crusts. Graininess is shown with the help of symbols, for instance, in dots or circles of different size.

A **snow column**, i.e. a scheme of snow profile section according to a chosen scale (vertical scale which reflects thickness of snow cover) is drawn for each described snow pit along the profile line. When drawing a profile it is recommended to select a uniform scale for all the snow shafts, whereas the columns are plotted below the relief line in the sites on the profile where descriptions have been carried out.

In order to make the snow cover scheme more pictorial, it can be expressed not only with the help of columns along the profile line but also with a firm line above the relief line (vertical scale which reflects

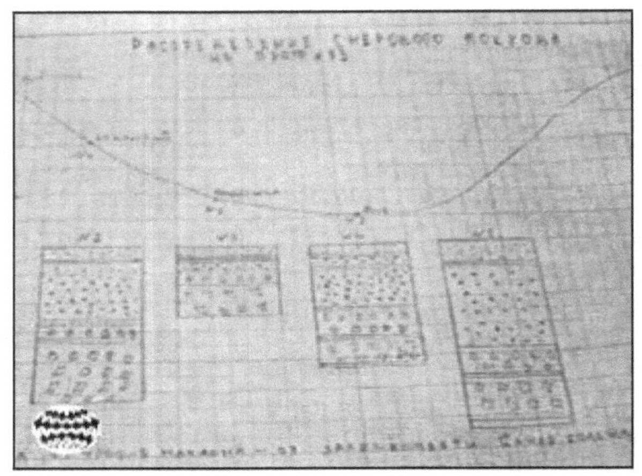

the total thickness of snow cover and is chosen arbitrarily). It can be done if descriptions have been carried out more or less evenly along the whole length of the profile (of course, extrapolating to sections between description sites). Such line will vividly show the total thickness of the snow cover along the profile line and, if vegetation is plotted on the profile drawing, it will allow to link regularities of snow cover distribution with previously studied landscape components – relief and vegetation.

Thus, the activity can result in drawing of a landscape profile scheme, where the following information is plotted: 1) relief line, 2) tree-and-shrubby vegetation; 3) line of the total thickness of the snow cover (along the whole length of the profile) and 4) columns/schemes of snow pit sections at different sites along the profile with detailed pictures of properties of different snow layers.

The following **questions** should be discussed in order to determine comprehension of fulfilled studies:

1. What is the general connection between the snow cover, relief and vegetation?

2. Besides total precipitation, what factors influence formation of the snow cover?

3. What role does the snow cover play in the lives of plants and animals (temperature, water reserve)?

4. It is necessary to reconstruct the course of weather conditions in the given winter (a number of thaws and snowfalls) and to answer the question: "How did vegetation and relief adjust weather peculiarities last winter in ways that are common for the given area?"